T0146970

MACAT

An Analysis of

Mahmood Mamdani's

Citizen and Subject

Contemporary Africa and the
Legacy of Late Colonialism

Meike de Goede

ROUTLEDGE

Published by Macat International Ltd
24:13 Coda Centre, 189 Munster Road, London SW6 6AW.

Distributed exclusively by Routledge
2 Park Square, Milton Park, Abingdon, Oxon OX14 4RN
711 Third Avenue, New York, NY 10017, USA

Routledge is an imprint of the Taylor & Francis Group, an informa business

www.macat.com
info@macat.com

Cataloguing in Publication Data
A catalogue record for this book is available from the British Library.
Library of Congress Cataloguing-in-Publication Data is available upon request.
Cover illustration: Etienne Gilfillan

ISBN 978-1-912302-72-7 (hardback)
ISBN 978-1-912128-69-3 (paperback)
ISBN 978-1-912281-60-2 (e-book)

Notice
The information in this book is designed to orientate readers of the work under analysis,
to elucidate and contextualise its key ideas and themes, and to aid in the development
of critical thinking skills. It is not meant to be used, nor should it be used, as a
substitute for original thinking or in place of original writing or research. References and
notes are provided for informational purposes and their presence does not constitute
endorsement of the information or opinions therein. This book is presented solely for
educational purposes. It is sold on the understanding that the publisher is not engaged
to provide any scholarly advice. The publisher has made every effort to ensure that
this book is accurate and up-to-date, but makes no warranties or representations with
regard to the completeness or reliability of the information it contains. The information
and the opinions provided herein are not guaranteed or warranted to produce particular
results and may not be suitable for students of every ability. The publisher shall not be
liable for any loss, damage or disruption arising from any errors or omissions, or from
the use of this book, including, but not limited to, special, incidental, consequential or
other damages caused, or alleged to have been caused, directly or indirectly, by the
information contained within.

CONTENTS

THE MACAT LIBRARY

The Macat Library is a series of unique academic explorations of seminal works in the humanities and social sciences – books and papers that have had a significant and widely recognised impact on their disciplines. It has been created to serve as much more than just a summary of what lies between the covers of a great book. It illuminates and explores the influences on, ideas of, and impact of that book. Our goal is to offer a learning resource that encourages critical thinking and fosters a better, deeper understanding of important ideas.

Each publication is divided into three Sections: Influences, Ideas, and Impact. Each Section has four Modules. These explore every important facet of the work, and the responses to it.

This Section-Module structure makes a Macat Library book easy to use, but it has another important feature. Because each Macat book is written to the same format, it is possible (and encouraged!) to cross-reference multiple Macat books along the same lines of inquiry or research. This allows the reader to open up interesting interdisciplinary pathways.

To further aid your reading, lists of glossary terms and people mentioned are included at the end of this book (these are indicated by an asterisk [*] throughout) – as well as a list of works cited.

Macat has worked with the University of Cambridge to identify the elements of critical thinking and understand the ways in which six different skills combine to enable effective thinking.
Three allow us to fully understand a problem; three more give us the tools to solve it. Together, these six skills make up the **PACIER** model of critical thinking. They are:

ANALYSIS – understanding how an argument is built
EVALUATION – exploring the strengths and weaknesses of an argument
INTERPRETATION – understanding issues of meaning

CREATIVE THINKING – coming up with new ideas and fresh connections
PROBLEM-SOLVING – producing strong solutions
REASONING – creating strong arguments

To find out more, visit **WWW.MACAT.COM.**

CRITICAL THINKING AND *CITIZEN AND SUBJECT*

Primary critical thinking skill: ANALYSIS
Secondary critical thinking skill: CREATIVE THINKING

Mahmood Mamdani's 1996 *Citizen and Subject* is a powerful work of analysis that lays bare the sources of the problems that plagued, and often still plague, African governments.

Analysis is one of the broadest and most fundamental critical thinking skills, and involves understanding the structure and features of arguments. Mamdani's strong analytical skills form the basis of an original investigation of the problems faced by the independent African governments in the wake of the collapse of the colonial regimes imposed by European powers such has Great Britain and France. It had long been clear that these newly-independent governments faced many problems – corruption, the imposition of anti-democratic rule, and many basic failures of day-to-day governance. They also tended to replicate many of the racially and ethnically prejudiced structures that were part of colonial rule. Mamdani analyses the many arguments about the sources of these problems, drawing out their hidden implications and assumptions in order to clear the way for his own creative new vision of the way to overcome the obstacles to democratization in Africa.

A dense and brilliant analysis of the true nature of colonialism's legacy in Africa, Mamdani's book remains influential to this day.

ABOUT THE AUTHOR OF THE ORIGINAL WORK

Mahmood Mamdani was born in Mumbai, India, in 1946, but was raised and educated in Uganda. President Idi Amin expelled his family in 1972, alongside all other Ugandans of Asian origin. Since then, Mamdani's glittering academic career has taken him to Tanzania, the United States, South Africa, and even back to Uganda. In 2008 he was voted among the top 10 public intellectuals by *Foreign Policy magazine*, while his essays have been published in the prestigious *London Review of Books*. He remains among Africa's foremost academics to this day.

ABOUT THE AUTHOR OF THE ANALYSIS

Dr Meike de Goede holds a PhD in international relations from the University of St Andrews, and is currently a university lecturer in African history at Leiden University. Her work focuses on the late colonial and early post-colonial period in French Equatorial Africa.

ABOUT MACAT

GREAT WORKS FOR CRITICAL THINKING

Macat is focused on making the ideas of the world's great thinkers accessible and comprehensible to everybody, everywhere, in ways that promote the development of enhanced critical thinking skills.

It works with leading academics from the world's top universities to produce new analyses that focus on the ideas and the impact of the most influential works ever written across a wide variety of academic disciplines. Each of the works that sit at the heart of its growing library is an enduring example of great thinking. But by setting them in context – and looking at the influences that shaped their authors, as well as the responses they provoked – Macat encourages readers to look at these classics and game-changers with fresh eyes. Readers learn to think, engage and challenge their ideas, rather than simply accepting them.

'Macat offers an amazing first-of-its-kind tool for interdisciplinary learning and research. Its focus on works that transformed their disciplines and its rigorous approach, drawing on the world's leading experts and educational institutions, opens up a world-class education to anyone.'

Andreas Schleicher
Director for Education and Skills, Organisation for Economic Co-operation and Development

'Macat is taking on some of the major challenges in university education ... They have drawn together a strong team of active academics who are producing teaching materials that are novel in the breadth of their approach.'

Prof Lord Broers,
former Vice-Chancellor of the University of Cambridge

'The Macat vision is exceptionally exciting. It focuses upon new modes of learning which analyse and explain seminal texts which have profoundly influenced world thinking and so social and economic development. It promotes the kind of critical thinking which is essential for any society and economy.
This is the learning of the future.'

Rt Hon Charles Clarke, former UK Secretary of State for Education

'The Macat analyses provide immediate access to the critical conversation surrounding the books that have shaped their respective discipline, which will make them an invaluable resource to all of those, students and teachers, working in the field.'

Professor William Tronzo, University of California at San Diego

WAYS IN TO THE TEXT

KEY POINTS

- Mahmood Mamdani is a prominent African scholar whose work has been influential in a number of academic disciplines.

- *Citizen and Subject: Contemporary Africa and the Legacy of Late Colonialism* argues that the current crisis of the African state* (that is, the state as it exists in Africa) is a consequence of the institutional legacy of colonialism.*

- *Citizen and Subject* is a historical narrative that explores the theoretical foundations of the modern African state and of contemporary conflict in Africa.

Who Is Mahmood Mamdani?

Mahmood Mamdani is a Ugandan of Indian origin. Born in Mumbai, India, in 1946, but raised and educated in Uganda, Mamdani and his family were expelled from the country by President Idi Amin* in 1972—along with all other Asians in Uganda—in what the dictator said was an attempt to nationalize the economy. Part of this process was to seize property from Asians and Europeans. The expulsion clearly became a key event in Mamdani's life, one that would deeply inform his work on postcolonial* Africa.

Mamdani's academic career took him to Tanzania, South Africa, and the United States. But that academic career was not without its problems. While working at the University of Cape Town in South Africa, Mamdani was suspended from the curriculum development committee over accusations he had made that the University was teaching about Africa from a European perspective, not an African one. This argument is central to his 1996 work, *Citizen and Subject: Contemporary Africa and the Legacy of Late Colonialism.*

Mamdani returned to Uganda in 1986 after Yoweri Museveni* ousted Milton Obote,* the dictator who had succeeded Amin in 1979. There, Mamdani chaired a Committee of Inquiry into the Local Governance System. That work on decentralizing power would feed into *Citizen and Subject.*

Mamdani is now Herbert Lehman Professor of Government in the department of anthropology and political science and the School of International and Public Affairs at Columbia University in New York. He is also director of the Makerere Institute of Social Research in Kampala, Uganda.

Mamdani has published other books on Africa since *Citizen and Subject* made him an academic star. In 2008, he was voted ninth top public intellectual by *Foreign Policy* magazine and remains among Africa's foremost academics to this day.

What Does *Citizen and Subject* Say?

Published in 1996, *Citizen and Subject* is a key work on the subject of how Africa has developed in the postcolonial period. It deals with the crisis of the African state and the reasons for that crisis.

Mamdani's main argument is that this crisis, which is the state's inability to deliver democratic governance, has its roots in Africa's colonial past rather than in any fundamental lack of ability of Africans to govern. He sets out to prove that inheriting a European structure of governance lies at the heart of Africa's current problems.

Mamdani identifies one of the main problems as a disconnect between the urban and the rural, a disconnect he maintains was reproduced from the days of colonial rule when urban and rural Africa were governed differently. In urban areas, there was direct rule based on modern law, while the rural areas were governed indirectly through more traditional authorities and laws based on customs. In urban areas people were treated as citizens, while in rural areas people were treated as subjects.

In *Citizen and Subject* Mamdani also argues that the concept of ethnicity*—the marker of identity that defines a group by common ancestral, social, cultural, and national experience—and the meaning it has in Africa today, is not something that is either traditional or natural. Rather, it is something created by European colonizers who constructed the idea to help them rule their African subjects. This construct of ethnicity became the root of resistance to colonial rule.

While Mamdani's arguments went against the grain of mainstream thinking on the crisis of the African state, his unique historic-institutional approach* gave his perspective great weight. He did not just spell out the problems facing modern Africa, he also traced those problems to their historic source: colonial rule.

Mamdani was, however, criticized for generalizing about the entire African continent based on two case studies—Uganda and South Africa—especially when South Africa was generally thought to be an exception within the African continent. Mamdani argued that on the contrary, South Africa, with its apartheid* system of racial segregation under a white minority rule was the *quintessential* African state.

Mamdani also became embroiled in a debate about how Africa was generally studied, arguing strongly that the continent should not be held up for comparison with Europe. He said that doing this would inevitably lead to conclusions that would never favor Africa, but would find it wanting. He preferred a perspective based on research gained from sources embedded in African communities.

Citizen and Subject was the book that made Mamdani's name and career. The themes of identity, conflict, and democratization—the transition from a non-democratic regime to a democratic one—would recur in his later works, but it is *Citizen and Subject* that most effectively highlights the important link between the legacy of colonialism and the challenges, failings, and conflicts of contemporary Africa.

Mamdani's status as a scholar was secured by controversial arguments about citizenship and conflict that he put forward in *Citizen and Subject*. These arguments are still relevant today and will be discussed for years to come. And it is hard to imagine that Mamdani's book will not be used as an important reference for those arguments.

Why Does *Citizen and Subject* Matter?

The subject of postcolonial Africa—its crisis of state, its conflicts, its problems with democratization—is complex and controversial. *Citizen and Subject* is an important work that goes to the heart of the subject, examining its history, its current status, and its future.

Mamdani may have gone against mainstream thinking in his analysis of the problems facing contemporary Africa, but his arguments are based on historical and sociological research gathered in the field. Yet his perspective on these problems is different. Instead of looking at Africa and comparing it with Europe, Mamdani sees Africa as separate, with its own historical path.

Citizen and Subject does not look at Africa as a project that has failed in European terms. Mamdani does not look at Africa as a continent with so many intrinsic weaknesses that it is destined to fail. Rather, he sees Africa as having inherited a failed colonial system that continued to fracture the African state.

For that reason, *Citizen and Subject* is an important exercise in how not to accept the parameters laid down by others. To get to the truth of a subject, it is sometimes necessary to break with an established tradition of research.

Citizen and Subject also teaches that comparing one system with another completely different one—in this case comparing Africa with Europe—is not always helpful in getting to the truth. Mamdani's conflict with the University of Cape Town in South Africa over how African history was taught highlights just how difficult it is to break away from Africa's colonial heritage. Mamdani's dispute with his academic peers over the "problematizing" of Africa was a real-life illustration of his point that you cannot look at Africa only in comparison with European history.

Mamdani did not agree with those who criticized his use of South Africa as an example in his arguments about the African continent. With its unique legal system of apartheid, South Africa was generally thought to be an exception to the rest of Africa. But Mamdani urged us to look beneath the surface of one particular legal system to discover the truth—that the whole of Africa was suffering under a similar hierarchy.

Apart from the insightful historical and social arguments it offers about the crisis of state in Africa and its causes, *Citizen and Subject* is also an exercise in thinking outside the box, of throwing out inherited systems to gain a deeper understanding.

SECTION 1
INFLUENCES

MODULE 1
THE AUTHOR AND THE HISTORICAL CONTEXT

KEY POINTS

- *Citizen and Subject* is an important work for students of contemporary Africa because it looks at the roots of the challenges facing the African state* — the building of the state, democracy, the way it is governed, its citizenship, and its civil conflict.

- Mahmood Mamdani's experiences in Uganda's turbulent post-independence era influenced the development of the central ideas of the book.

- *Citizen and Subject* was published in the context of political change on the African continent. It took on board new concerns about recurring problems, such as a deteriorating economic situation and civil war.

Why Read This Text?

Published in 1996, Mahmood Mandani's *Citizen and Subject: Contemporary Africa and the Legacy of Late Colonialism* is a provocative contribution to the debate about the crisis of the African state in the late twentieth century. It challenges the argument that this crisis is homegrown and the consequence of poor government by arguing that the crisis is, in fact, a result of the institutional legacy of colonialism.*

So what exactly was this crisis of the African state in the late twentieth century? After the publication of *Citizen and Subject,* Africa continued to see state failure* — the inability of a state to complete its core tasks — and violent conflict. But the book helps us to understand

> ❝ [*Citizen and Subject*] was a book I wrote at a time
> when, really, there were few certainties. The Cold War
> had ended. There was no one big idea. The situation
> we were used to, the big issues, were settled ... The
> challenge was to think of political reform. Try and think
> of politics in some autonomous way. It was a book that
> was a response to that—an attempt to step back and
> think about the previous two decades. ❞
>
> Mahmood Mamdani, "In Conversation With Mahmood Mamdani" in
> *Warscapes* online magazine (www.warscapes.com)

the historic roots of what is happening in Africa today. Mamdani
argues that the problems Africa faces—such as citizenship,
democratization,* and civil conflict—have their origins in the
continent's colonial past.

A year after it was published, *Citizen and Subject* won the prestigious
African Studies Association Herskovits Prize for the best book on
Africa[1] and has since been named as one of the 100 best African books
of the twentieth century.[2] Mamdani was voted ninth top public
intellectual by the influential US magazine *Foreign Policy* in 2008.[3]

Author's Life

Mahmood Mamdani was born in Mumbai, India, in 1946, and grew
up in Uganda. He was educated in both Uganda and the United States
before working at academic institutions in Uganda, Tanzania, South
Africa, and the United States.

His career path was somewhat dictated by political events in
Uganda. In 1972, when Mamdani was 26, Ugandan President Idi
Amin* expelled Asians living in the country. This Asian expulsion*
was a part of Amin's desire to nationalize the Ugandan economy and
effectively place it in the hands of the people he saw as "indigenous" to

the country. After a short time spent in a refugee camp in the United Kingdom, Mamdani moved to Tanzania in 1973 to teach at the University of Dar es Salaam. A war between Uganda and neighboring Tanzania eventually saw Amin being ousted from power and replaced by Yoweri Museveni* in 1980. Mamdani finally returned to Uganda in 1986, where he chaired a Committee of Inquiry into the Local Governance System. The inquiry worked through public consultations to advise the new Museveni government how to strengthen decentralization and move power away from central government towards a more localized democracy.[4] This experience piqued Mamdani's interest in the persistent African problem of the urban-rural divide* and laid the roots for ideas he would later develop in *Citizen and Subject*.

In 1996 Mamdani was offered the opportunity to work at the University of Cape Town at the Centre for African Studies. This led to what became known as the "Mamdani Affair." Shortly after the publication of *Citizen and Subject*, Mamdani was suspended from the curriculum development committee at the university over a disagreement about his syllabus for the course, "Problematizing Africa."[5] He criticized the Centre for teaching from a colonial perspective and for accepting a colonial historic timeline of Africa. Mamdani suggested that the Centre for African Studies was, in fact, a new "Home for Bantu Education," making reference to the 1953 piece of legislation that had enforced the country's apartheid* education system of racially segregated facilities.[6] The matter was discussed in a public seminar at the University of Cape Town[7] and a special issue of the African studies journal *Social Dynamics* was dedicated to the controversy.[8]

Not long afterwards, Mamdani left Cape Town and moved to Columbia University in New York. He is currently Herbert Lehman Professor of Government in the department of anthropology and political science and the School of International and Public Affairs at

Columbia University, while also holding the role of Director of the Makerere Institute of Social Research, in Kampala, Uganda.

Author's Background

The end of the Cold War* between the United States and the Soviet Union* in 1989 led to a wind of political change blowing through the African continent. This change was a part of what had already been dubbed the Third Wave of Democratization.* This third wave had started with the collapse of military dictatorships in southern Europe in the mid-1970s and was followed by those in Eastern Europe and Africa at the end of the 1980s.[9] But it was not long before critical voices started to question the nature of these political changes. The move towards democratization included the introduction of elections, for example, but critics suggested that simply holding elections did not necessarily mean that democratic regimes were actually being set up.[10] Some scholars argued that civil political rights,* such as the right to free speech and religious freedom, were often blatantly disrespected,[11] while corruption and patrimonial politics*—running government based on personal relations and friendships—were still rife. Political reform existed in appearance only.[12] The critics said it was difficult to find any signs of good governance* in Africa.[13]

Added to this, there were problems with structural adjustment programs* geared towards market reform and capitalist development. The idea was that the economies of African states would be transformed into liberal market economies. But many African countries instead became heavily indebted and regimes were significantly weakened.[14] In some countries civil war broke out and the states failed.[15]

In looking at the crises in the African state, Mamdani's *Citizen and Subject* draws mainly on two case studies, Uganda and South Africa. In both countries, the 1990s were interesting times politically. In Uganda, President Museveni resisted pressures to democratize, arguing that democratization would mean politics would be played out along ethnic identity lines, increasing divisions among ethnic groups in the country. To his mind, democratization would be a threat to the fragile stability of a country already battered by decades of dictatorship and civil war. Museveni argued that Uganda's economy and social structures should be rebuilt first and certainly before gradual political reforms could take place.[16]

In South Africa, meanwhile, the early 1990s had brought radical political change. The country had joined the Third Wave of Democratization as apartheid was abolished in 1991 and the first general elections were organized in 1994.[17] This was a major turning point for the country. Mamdani visited South Africa on several occasions between 1991 and 1993, conducting research on how control had been exerted under apartheid. He was struck by the similarities between South Africa's apartheid administration and the rural colonial administration in other African countries under French or British rule.[18] This recognition drove Mamdani's core concepts for his forthcoming book, and *Citizen and Subject* was published in the context of turbulent times on the African continent. It was a time of hope for real change and a more prosperous future, but also a time of concern about recurring problems, deteriorating economies, and civil war.

NOTES

1   "J. Melville Herskovits Award," African Studies Association, accessed January 2, 2015, http://www.africanstudies.org/awards-prizes/herskovits-award.

2   "Africa's 100 best books of the 20th Century," African Studies Centre, accessed February 11, 2015, http://www.ascleiden.nl/content/webdossiers/africas-100-best-books-20th-century.

3   Anonymous, "The World's Top 20 Public Intellectuals," *Foreign Policy* 167 (2008): 54–7.

4   Ministry of Local Government. *Report of the Commission of Inquiry into the Local Government System* (Kampala, 1987).

5   Isaac A. Kamola, "Pursuing Excellence in a World-Class University: the Mamdani Affairs and the Politics of Global Higher Education," *Journal of Higher Education in Africa* 9, nos. 1 and 2 (2011): 128.

6   Mahmood Mamdani, "Is African Studies to be Turned Into a New Home for Bantu Education at UCT?" Text of remarks by Professor Mahmood Mamdani at the Seminar on the Africa Core of the Foundation Course for the Faculty of Social Sciences and Humanities, University of Cape Town, April 22, 1998.

7   Seminar on the Africa Core of the Foundation Course for the Faculty of Social Sciences and Humanities, University of Cape Town, April 22, 1998.

8   Johan Muller, "Editorial Introduction," *Social Dynamics* 24, no. 2 (1998): 1–6; Mahmood Mamdani, "Teaching Africa at the Post-Apartheid University of Cape Town: A Critical View of the 'Introduction to Africa' Core Course in the Social Science and Humanities Faculty's Foundation Semester, 1998," *Social Dynamics* 24, no. 2 (1998): 1–32; Nadia Hartman, "Discussion of Certain Aspects of Mamdani's Paper: Teaching Africa at the Post-Apartheid University of Cape Town," *Social Dynamics* 24, no. 2 (1998): 33–9; Martin Hall, "Teaching Africa at the Post–Apartheid University of Cape Town: A Response," *Social Dynamics* 24, no. 2 (1998): 40–62; Mahmood Mamdani, "Is African Studies to be Turned Into a New Home for Bantu Education at UCT?" *Social Dynamics* 24, no. 2 (1998): 63–75; Johann Graaff, "Pandering to Pedagogy or Consumed by Content: Brief Thoughts on Mahmood Mamdani's 'Teaching at the Post-Apartheid University of Cape Town'," *Social Dynamics* 24, no. 2 (1998): 76–85; Martin Hall, "'Bantu Education'? A Reply to Mahmood Mamdani," *Social Dynamics* 24, no. 2 (1998): 86–92.

9   Samuel P. Huntington, *The Third Wave: Democratization in the Late Twentieth Century* (Norman, OK: University of Oklahoma Press, 1991), 287.

10   Andreas Schedler, "The Menu of Manipulation," *Journal of Democracy* 13, no. 2 (2002): 42; Adam Przeworski et al, "What Makes Democracies Endure?" *Journal of Democracy* 7, no. 1 (1996): 39–55.

11   Maxwell Owosu, "Democracy and Africa? A View from the Village," *Journal of Modern African Studies* 30, no. 3 (1992): 384; Gabrielle Lynch and Gordon Crawford. "Democratization in Africa 1990–2010: An Assessment," *Democratization* 18, no. 2 (2011): 280.

12   Patrick Chabal and Jean-Pascal Daloz, *Africa Works: Disorder as Political Instrument* (Oxford: James Currey, 1999), 37–8; Michael Bratton and Nicolas van de Walle, *Democratic Experiments in Africa: Regime Transitions in Comparative Perspective* (Cambridge University Press: 1997), 63.

13   Bruce Baker, "The Class of 1990: How Have the Autocratic Leaders of Sub-Saharan Africa Fared under Democratisation?" *Third World Quarterly* 19, no. 1 (1998): 126.

14 Richard Jeffries, "The state, structural adjustment and good government in Africa," Journal of Commonwealth and Comparative Politics 31, no. 3 (1993): 20–35; Julius E. Nyang'oro, "The Evolving Role of the African State under Structural Adjustment," in *Beyond Structural Adjustment in Africa: the Political Economy of Sustainable and Democratic Development*, eds. Julius E. Nyang'oro and Timothy M. Shaw (New York: Praeger, 1992), 21.

15 Robert I. Rotberg, "The Failure and Collapse of Nation-States: Breakdown, Prevention, and Repair," in *When States Fail: Causes and Consequences*, ed. Robert I. Rotberg (Princeton, NJ: Princeton University Press, 2004), 47.

16 Das, Anil Kumar, "The Reluctant Democrat: Museveni and the Future of Democracy in Uganda," *Africa Quarterly* 39, no. 4 (1999): 61.

17 Robert Ross, *A Concise History of South Africa. Second Edition.* (Cambridge: Cambridge University Press, 2008), 200–11.

18 Mahmood Mamdani, *Citizen and Subject: Contemporary Africa and the Legacy of Late Colonialism* (Princeton, NJ: Princeton University Press, 1996), 7.

MODULE 2
ACADEMIC CONTEXT

KEY POINTS

- African Studies is a field of study mainly—but not exclusively—located within the social sciences and humanities. It aims to understand events and processes in Africa.

- Africanists typically use a range of disciplinary approaches, including those from political science, anthropology, history, economics, law, sociology, geography, culture, literature, and languages.

- Mamdani is trained in political science, law, and governance studies, but his work is multidisciplinary, combining politics, history, law, and anthropology.

The Work in its Context

Mahmood Mamdani's *Citizen and Subject: Contemporary Africa and the Legacy of Late Colonialism* is a work that should be located in the broad field of African Studies, which is not a discipline in its own right. As with other "area studies," such as Latin American Studies and Asian Studies, it is a field of scholarly interest in social phenomena from a specific geographical area. As such, it should be mainly placed in the fields of the liberal arts, or humanities, and social sciences, though not exclusively so.

Africanists typically undertake multidisciplinary* and interdisciplinary* work—combining research methods and approaches from different disciplines. African studies can include political science, anthropology, history, economics, law, sociology, geography, culture, literature, and languages. This means the field of African Studies is very broad and hard to define by anything other

❝ This is an argument not against comparative study but against those who would dehistoricize phenomena by lifting them from context, whether in the name of an abstract universalism or of an intimate particularism, only to make sense of them by analogy. ❞

Mahmood Mamdani, *Citizen and Subject*

than a shared interest in a geographical area. Mamdani himself is educated in political science, law, and governance studies. His work, however, is interdisciplinary and is informed by insights gained from political science, law, history, and anthropology.

Overview of the Field

Contemporary African Studies goes back to the work of the early anthropologists studying human behavior at the beginning of the twentieth century. These scholars found little written material on African societies, and colonial powers had limited understanding of how African societies functioned, plus there were deep cultural differences between Western scholars and the Africans they studied. For these reasons, research into what was happening in African society meant using approaches that would get to the heart of Africans' lives. In other words, anthropological approaches emphasized long-term research embedded in societies to develop a deep understanding of how those societies operated. Anthropologists such as Edward Evans-Pritchard* studied African societies in-depth and on the ground to bring a whole new understanding of those societies and how they functioned politically.[1]

The historian Jan Vansina* is another influential academic who has contributed to the development of African Studies as an interdisciplinary field of research. Vansina studied oral traditions and oral history—the way a society's history is recorded through storytelling—in Equatorial Africa,[*2] particularly in the area currently known as the Democratic Republic of Congo. Because he based his work on oral sources* Vansina challenged academic conventions of historiography*—or the study of the writing of history—that suggested only written historical sources were valid.

Studies such as these laid the groundwork for further research on African societies and social circumstances. They have also contributed to the development of African Studies as a recognized multidisciplinary academic field. Mamdani's work, especially *Citizen and Subject*, builds on these traditions, which combine different methods of research to offer a view of a subject that recognizes its complexity.

Academic Influences

Mamdani's direct influences are not so obvious, even if his work is clearly influenced by African Studies researchers who use multiple disciplines to build a picture of a society and its history. This is perhaps most obvious in Mamdani's rejection of history by analogy.[*3] History by analogy means using what happened in Western history as a model for social, political, and economic development in other regions. The histories of Africa and other parts of the world are then measured against this model. This rejection of history by analogy is not itself a theme in the book, but it is outlined in the book's introduction, where Mamdani states: "This is an argument not against comparative study but against those who would dehistoricize phenomena by lifting them from context, whether in the name of an abstract universalism or of an intimate particularism, only to make sense of them by analogy."[4]

Mamdani rejects using examples and models from Europe to give meaning to African political history. Such an approach would look for what Africa lacks and then for what Africa should become in order to follow Western examples. Instead, Mamdani looks at the current crisis of governance in Africa from the point of view of Africa's own history.[5] He does not tell the story of Africa by comparing it with the history of

Europe. Instead, *Citizen and Subject* is structured around experiences that are specific to the history of the African state.* Mamdani focuses on colonialism and the structures of rule that colonialism produced and that postcolonial African states inherited. For him, the essence of his work lies where structures of power and structures of resistance meet, both in the colonial and postcolonial era.

This way of looking at non-Western societies from the point of view of non-Western peoples is also characteristic of postcolonial studies* and subaltern studies.* Postcolonial studies emphasize persistent dominant structures between the former colonizers and the former colonized, while subaltern studies* examine the historic experiences of dominated and suppressed people. Mamdani's work should also be seen in the context of these theoretical debates.

NOTES

1   Edward E. Evans-Pritchard, *Witchcraft, Oracles, and Magic Among the Azande* (Oxford: Oxford University Press, 1937); Edward E. Evans-Pritchard, *The Nuer: A Description of the Modes of Livelihood and Political Institutions of a Nilotic People* (Oxford: Clarendon Press, 1940).

2   Jan Vansina, *Paths in the Rainforest: Toward a History of Political Tradition in Equatorial Africa* (Madison: University of Wisconsin Press, 1990); Jan Vansina, *Oral Tradition as History* (London: James Currey, 1985).

3   Mahmood Mamdani, *Citizen and Subject: Contemporary Africa and the Legacy of Late Colonialism* (Princeton, NJ: Princeton University Press, 1996), 9–10.

4   Mamdani, *Citizen and Subject,* 13.

5   Mamdani, *Citizen and Subject*, 9–10.

MODULE 3
THE PROBLEM

KEY POINTS

- *Citizen and Subject* is concerned with understanding the causes of the crisis of the African state,* and examining routes to explore for more successful democratization* and sustainable development.

- Mainstream arguments held that the current crisis of the African state was homegrown or a consequence of the exogenous — or "imported" — nature of the state in Africa.

- Mamdani rejects these arguments and argues that the crisis of the African state is rooted in the institutional legacy of colonialism.*

Core Question

Mahmood Mamdani's *Citizen and Subject: Contemporary Africa and the Legacy of Late Colonialism* is an investigation into the nature of power in the postcolonial African state—a state that was in crisis in the late twentieth century. The end of the Cold War* in 1989 gave rise to great political change on the continent, known as the Third Wave of Democratization* in Africa.[1] *Citizen and Subject* addresses concerns such as those expressed by political scientist Crawford Young,* who said that "the euphoria that accompanied the arrival of the third wave in Africa has long since evaporated."[2] The optimism of the Third Wave of Democratization made way for the pessimism of the crisis of the African state. In the context of these emerging concerns, Mamdani's research question became urgent. His work aims to understand this crisis on a fundamental level and approaches the crisis of governance in Africa from both a historic and an institutional perspective. Focusing

> ❝ [The contemporary state in sub-Saharan Africa] descends from arbitrary colonial administrative units designed as instruments of domination, oppression and exploitation. No doubt after some 40 years of independence these states have been transformed, adopted, adapted, endogenised* [developed from within]. Yet, their origins remain exogenous [originating from outside]: European, not African, and set up against African societies rather than having evolved out of the relationships of groups and individuals in societies. ❞
>
> Pierre Englebert, "The Contemporary African State: Neither African Nor State"

on the history of the state in Africa, he identifies the current crisis of governance as the outcome of Africa's (post)colonial history. The book directly links Africa's colonial experience and the current crisis of state and governance, something that went against the grain of contemporary thinking.

The Participants

Mamdani wanted his book to address the following issues, which he saw as urgent:

- The crisis of state and governance
- The difficult process of democratization in Africa
- Persistent underdevelopment and economic stagnation.

These themes were as interesting to scholars at the time when Mamdani was researching them as they are now. Some thought the way governments were run in Africa was responsible for the crisis of the state, meaning that the crisis was, in fact, homegrown.[3] Crawford Young argued that ethnicity,* religion, and race caused splits in

African society and that weak governance worsened the splits.[4] Others have argued that patrimonial* governance—government where leaders encouraged more of a patron-client relationship—were still deep rooted despite democratic reform. This suggested that the problem of governance in Africa was a result of its own longstanding political culture.[5]

The French sociologist Jean-Francois Bayart* was an influential figure in this debate. In his 1993 book, *The State in Africa: the Politics of the Belly*, Bayart suggested that "the social struggles which make up the quest for hegemony and the production of the state bear the hallmarks of the rush for spoils in which all actors—rich and poor—participate in the world of networks."[6] For Bayart, this rush for spoils at all levels of society as a fundamental element of sociopolitical struggle helps us understand corruption, state violence, and ethnic conflict in Africa. Others have argued that the main cause of the crisis in the African state is external, rather than African. The modern state originated in Europe, and was exported to Africa by Europeans through colonialism, then imported by Africans through independence. Political scientist Bertrand Badie* has argued that in this process, the state has lost its original meaning, and has gone on to acquire new meaning in a new context.[7] Jean-Francois Bayart has called this process "grafting," by which he refers to the establishment of a political structure on top of social structures that are different from those in the place the political structure originates. The fact that the social structures are different means that the state will function differently in this new environment.[8] For historian Basil Davidson,* the adoption of the ideas and understanding of the Western state was necessary for African states to gain independence, but has been a curse for African societies ever since.[9]

The Contemporary Debate

Mamdani's main concern was that mainstream studies on problems of contemporary African states skate over the complexity of the

African context without fully understanding it. Here, he was talking in particular of the institutional legacy of colonialism and the idea of ethnicity.

Badie, Bayart, and Davidson focused their ideas about the crisis of the African state on the practices of governance: the way in which the state was run. Mamdani, however, was interested in the *structures* of governance and the historic roots of these practices. It was not simply a question of *how* the state was governed, but *why* the governing structures were set up in the way they were.

"In grappling with the question of democracy and governance," Mamdani writes, "I have both shifted perspective from the mode of livelihood to the mode of rule and argued that there is a historical specificity to the mode of rule on the African continent."[10] It's in this unique way that *Citizen and Subject* challenges mainstream ideas on the crisis of the African state and governance in Africa. It looks at the nature of power in Africa from a historical perspective and sees it as a product of colonialism tangled up with ethnicity issues and the way government institutions have traditionally functioned.

To challenge these mainstream ideas, Mamdani focuses on three questions. First, to what extent was the power structure in contemporary Africa shaped by the colonial period? Second, to what extent is ethnicity a dimension of the power structure as well as a dimension of resistance to that power structure? And third, if power reproduced itself by exaggerating difference and denying the existence of an oppressed majority, doesn't protest need to transcend these differences without denying them?[11] These questions were different from traditional questions guiding research on governance practices in Africa. So *Citizen and Subject* not only challenges mainstream ideas, but also draws attention to different dynamics.

NOTES

1   Samuel P. Huntington, *The Third Wave: Democratization in the Late Twentieth Century* (Norman: University of Oklahoma Press, 1991), 287.

2   Crawford Young, "The Third Wave of Democratization in Africa: Ambiguities and Contradictions," in *State, Conflict and Democracy,* ed. Richard Joseph (Boulder, CO: Lynne Rienner, 1999), 25.

3   Robert H. Bates, *When Things Fell Apart. State Failure in Late-Century Africa.* (Cambridge: Cambridge University Press, 2008), 52–3.

4   Young, "The Third Wave," 25.

5   Patrick Chabal and Jean-Pascal Daloz, *Africa Works: Disorder as Political Instrument* (Oxford: James Currey, 1999), 37–8; Michael Bratton and Nicolas van de Walle, *Democratic Experiments in Africa: Regime Transitions in Comparative Perspective* (Cambridge: Cambridge University Press: 1997), 63.

6   Jean-François Bayart, *The State in Africa: The Politics of the Belly* (London: Longman, 1993), 235.

7   Bertrand Badie, *The Imported State: The Westernisation of Political Order*, trans. Claudia Royal (Stanford, CA: Stanford University Press, 2000).

8   Jean-François Bayart, "L'historicité de l'État importé," in *La greffe de l'état*, ed. Jean-François Bayart (Paris: Karthala, 1996).

9   Basil Davidson, *The Black Man's Burden: Africa and the Curse of the Nation-State* (Oxford: James Currey, 1992).

10   Mahmood Mamdani, *Citizen and Subject: Contemporary Africa and the Legacy of Late Colonialism* (Princeton, NJ: Princeton University Press, 1996), 294.

11   Mamdani, *Citizen and Subject*, 7–8.

MODULE 4
THE AUTHOR'S CONTRIBUTION

KEY POINTS

- According to Mamdani, the main obstacle to democratization* and good governance* in Africa is the fundamental disconnect between the urban and rural populations and the dual systems of governance of these two groups.

- *Citizen and Subject* draws attention to structural, long-term, and often overlooked aspects of the nature of power in postcolonial Africa, particularly the institutional legacy of colonialism* and the complexities of traditional governance that co-exist within the modern state.

- Mamdani put forward the original idea that the apartheid* structure of South Africa was not an exception in Africa, but was rather a perfect representation of a colonial state.

Author's Aims

When Mahmood Mamdani wrote *Citizen and Subject* it was a turbulent time on the African continent and there was a lot of interest in trying to understand both the African state* and African governance. Why did states fail to deliver development, stability, economic growth, and general well-being to African people after independence?[1] This debate was dominated by what Mamdani referred to as "Afro-pessimists"[2]—those who thought Africa's current crisis was homegrown, the result of local factors such as African political customs and traditions. Mamdani wanted to develop an argument to challenge those mainstream ideas about Africa's current situation. He felt Afro-pessimists did not fully grasp Africa's specific difficulties in their proper historic contexts. In *Citizen and Subject,* Mamdani makes the connection between the

> ❝ The point of this book is that any effective opposition in practice, and any theoretical analysis that would lead to one, must link the rural and the urban in ways that have not been done. ❞
>
> Mahmood Mamdani, *Citizen and Subject*

institutional legacy of colonialism and the contemporary crisis of African governance absolutely clear. He believed Africa's structures of governance were riddled with the institutional legacy of colonialism and those structures had produced a rural-urban divide. Mamdani wanted to argue that the reason democratization in Africa had failed up to that point was because the structures of governance in place continued to reflect the rule of the colonial predecessors.

Because Mamdani challenges assumptions that are generally applied to the whole continent, he provides an analysis of the whole African continent as well. The aim of the book is not to show that there are cases that cannot be understood through mainstream ideas, but to challenge the mainstream ideas as a whole.

Approach

To develop the argument about the institutional legacy of colonialism, *Citizen and Subject* challenges four mainstream ideas. First, Mamdani criticizes the way African Studies researchers write the history of Africa by comparing it with the history of Europe.[3] This is history by analogy.* Mamdani counters so-called development theory,* which measures African reality against European history. This takes African reality out of its own context and process.[4] *Citizen and Subject* provides a perspective on the African state and its history from an African point of view, not a European one.

Second, Mamdani challenges the idea that South Africa is an exception to the general rule in Africa. He argues that although apartheid is generally considered a specific feature of South Africa's history alone, it is actually typical of the African colonial state. Mamdani argues that apartheid was an answer to the same "native question" that colonial authorities grappled with all over Africa: how can a minority of Europeans govern over a large majority native population? In doing so, he aims to bring South Africa back to the field of African Studies, which had tended to exclude the country as an exception, rather than as a part of the general history of the continent.

Third, Mamdani sets out to "underline the contradictory character of ethnicity.*"[5] The argument that ethnicity in the way we have come to understand it is a colonial construct and an instrument for oppression has also been made by others. The argument runs that colonial rulers assumed ethnic groups, or "tribes," were static and neatly defined identity groups ruled by a chief, whereas in reality ethnic identity was much more fluid and dynamic in pre-colonial times.[6] Mamdani argues that ethnicity is a more complex issue. For him, ethnicity's contradictory character lies in the fact that on the one hand it was used as a tool for colonial domination of the rural population, while on the other it also became the structure that defined resistance towards colonial power.[7]

Finally, Mamdani sets out to show that the bifurcated state* created by colonialism may have been deracialized—in that rulers were not of a different race—but was not democratized after independence. The bifurcated state is a term coined by Mamdani to refer to the legal and administrative division—rural and urban—of the colonial state. And here is where the obstacle for the transition to democracy lies. Postcolonial reform only created new versions of the existing structures of despotism,* where government power is concentrated in a single, often tyrannical, individual.

With these four ideas at its heart, to examine the meeting point between power and resistance the book is divided in two parts, the first focusing on the structure of power and the second on the forms of resistance it enables.

Contribution in Context

The concepts and themes Mamdani explores in *Citizen and Subject* are not specific to him. But he did think about how these common themes made sense in the historical, political, and social context of Africa. This in turn helped him develop new insights into and new interpretations of those common themes.

Mamdani develops an interpretation of the concept of ethnic identity, claiming it as an idea and a structure that colonial rulers used in order to govern. This reading of ethnic identity was very different from commonly held ideas in Africa, where ethnic identity is seen either as a natural, ancient phenomenon[8] or as a concept created by society.[9]

Mamdani also reconfigures our understanding of the colonial legacy. The idea that postcolonial Africa is faced with a colonial legacy in economic, political, psychological, and cultural terms is well established. However, Mamdani puts forward the idea that this colonial legacy is still present in a country's institutions of governance. In other words, the structures set up to govern a state in modern Africa are riddled with traditions left over from colonial times. This focus on institutions of governance also allows Mamdani to make another original claim, that apartheid South Africa was not an exception on the African continent, but rather represented the quintessential colonial state.

NOTES

1   Some prominent works in this debate, besides *Citizen and Subject*, are: Jean-François Bayart, *The State in Africa: The Politics of the Belly* (London: Longman, 1993); Jean-François Bayart et al., *The Criminalisation of the State in Africa* (Oxford: James Currey, 1999); Patrick Chabal, *Power in Africa: An Essay in Political Interpretation* (New York: St Martin's Press, 1992); Patrick Chabal and Jean-Pascal Daloz, *Africa Works: Disorder as Political Instrument* (Oxford: James Currey, 1999); Jeffrey Herbst, *States and Power in Africa: Comparative Lessons in Authority and Control* (Princeton, NJ: Princeton University Press, 2000); William Reno, *Warlord Politics and African States* (Boulder, CO: Lynne Rienner,1998).

2   Mahmood Mamdani, *Citizen and Subject: Contemporary Africa and the Legacy of Late Colonialism* (Princeton, NJ: Princeton University Press, 1996), 285.

3   Mamdani, *Citizen and Subject*, 8.

4   Mamdani, *Citizen and Subject*, 12.

5   Mamdani, *Citizen and Subject*, 8.

6   See on this topic for example: Bayart, *The State in Africa*; Bruce Berman, "Ethnicity, Patronage and the African State: The Politics of Uncivil Nationalism," *African Affairs* 97, no. 388 (1998): 305–41; Bruce Berman and John Lonsdale, *Unhappy Valley: Conflict in Kenya and Africa* (Oxford: James Currey, 1992); Chabal, *Power in Africa;* Chabal and Daloz, *Africa Works*; Frederick Cooper, *Colonialism in Question: Theory, Knowledge, History* (Berkeley: University of California Press, 2005); Terence Ranger, "The Invention of Tradition in Colonial Africa," in *The Invention of Tradition*, eds. E. J. Hobsbawm and Terence Ranger (Cambridge: Cambridge University Press, 1993).

7   Mamdani, *Citizen and Subject*, 185.

8   Pierre Van den Berghe, "Does Race Matter?" in *Ethnicity*, eds. John Hutchinson and Anthony D. Smith (Oxford: Oxford University Press, 1996).

9   Kanchan Chandra, "Cumulative Findings in the Study of Ethnic Politics," *APSA-CP Newsletter* 12, no. 1 (2001): 7–11; Benedict Anderson, *Imagined Communities: Reflections on the Origin and Spread of Nationalism* (New York: Verso, 1991).

SECTION 2
IDEAS

MAIN IDEAS

KEY POINTS

- The key themes of *Citizen and Subject* are the crisis in the African state,* how state power is structured, the institutional legacy of colonialism,* and the governing differences between urban and rural areas.

- Mamdani says that in postcolonial Africa, the fundamental distinction between rural and urban rule that was characteristic of the colonial state has been reproduced. This disconnect between urban and rural is the main obstacle to successful democratization.*

- First, Mamdani develops his argument about the structure of power, showing how the bifurcated state* was institutionally designed and then reproduced after colonialism. The second part of the book considers forms of resistance to it. Putting the two sections together, Mamdani argues how both the institutional legacy of colonialism and the forms of resistance it generated reproduced the bifurcated state.

Key Themes

Mahmood Mamdani's *Citizen and Subject: Contemporary Africa and the Legacy of Late Colonialism* aims to provide an understanding of the crisis in the way Africa was governed in the late twentieth century. Mamdani argues that this crisis and the way politics functions in Africa is rooted in the institutional legacy of colonialism, which persists in the governing structures of the contemporary African state.[1] The fundamental disconnect between the way urban and rural areas are governed is the essence of the institutional legacy of colonialism.[2]

> ❝ In grappling with the question of democracy and governance, I have both shifted perspective from the mode of livelihood to the mode of rule and argued that there is a historical specificity to the mode of rule on the African continent. ❞
>
> Mahmood Mamdani, *Citizen and Subject*

Whereas in urban areas people were governed as citizens, in rural areas people were governed as subjects. This has defined the systems of rule, as well as the structures of popular resistance to this rule.[3] So in contemporary Africa there remains a clear distinction between citizens and subjects, resulting in a fundamental sociopolitical split among social groups.

Mamdani criticizes mainstream arguments that aim to blame the problematic state in Africa on the way the state has been governed by postcolonial regimes. Although Mamdani does not deny that many African countries have been poorly governed during the postcolonial era, for him this is a symptom, not a cause of the problematic nature of the African state. For Mamdani, the problem lies in the institutional design of the state, not in how individual regimes and people have governed within that design. The problem is with the inherited colonial system, not with the way that postcolonial African governments have used it.

Exploring the Ideas

The institutional legacy of colonialism can be found in what Mamdani labels the "bifurcated state" and in "decentralized despotism."* The bifurcated state refers to the colonial division—both legal and administrative—between the governance of rural subjects and urban citizens. The urban areas were ruled by a modern European system of administration and law, while the rural areas were governed by more traditional laws and administration.[4] Mamdani describes the system of rule over the rural areas as decentralized despotism, where despotic colonial rule was mediated through traditional authorities* such as chiefs and kings. Mamdani argues that these traditional authorities were not necessarily as traditional as they seemed. In fact, they were often either freshly imposed or somehow reconstituted to create a local hierarchy.[5] Mamdani says that the postcolonial state* has simply reproduced this system of rule, rather than getting rid of it.[6]

After setting out this structure of power, Mamdani uses the second part of the book to look at how forms of resistance and protest were shaped by the parameters set by the structures of power. Mamdani draws mainly on two examples: peasant resistance in rural Uganda and migrant workers in urban South Africa.

The two parts of the book—one on power and one on resistance— combine to illustrate Mamdani's point that the colonial bifurcated state was reproduced in the postcolonial era.[7] He argues that the state was deracialized, but not democratized, and that the fundamental disconnect between urban and rural populations and their dual systems of government were the main obstacles to democratization and good governance in Africa.[8]

Mamdani argues that for democratization to be successful in Africa, linking urban and rural governance is essential. This linking, he says, will help overcome divisions in the African state between citizens and subjects, between rights and customs,* between participation and representation, and between civil society* and community.

Language and Expression

Mamdani expresses his argument by shaping the book in two distinct parts. In the first part of the book, Mamdani discusses the construction of the bifurcated state, decentralized despotism (where authoritarian central rule is dispensed through local set-ups), postcolonial reform, and the way the colonial structure was simply reproduced rather than dismantled. In three consecutive chapters, Mamdani discusses the three main pillars of decentralized despotism. These are indirect rule,* the opposing forces of civil and customary* power, and the economy of indirect rule. Each chapter analyses the emergence, as well as the limits, of postcolonial reform.

In the book's second part, Mamdani considers how resistance and protest emerges from this power structure, primarily by looking at two case studies, the peasants in rural Uganda and the migrant workers in South Africa.

Although the structure of the book is accessible, *Citizen and Subject* is still challenging as a piece of scholarly work. It is highly theoretical and the language it uses is conceptual, relating more to ideas than facts. Mamdani develops several complex concepts, but it is vital to understand them to grasp the depth of his arguments. The main argument is most clearly explained in the introduction, and *Citizen and Subject* is not a book where the chapters stand on their own. This is because Mamdani's arguments spread out over the full length of the work.

NOTES

1   Jean-François Bayart, *Les études postcoloniales: Un carnaval académique* (Paris: Karthala, 2010); Jean-François Bayart, *The State in Africa: The Politics of the Belly* (London: Longman, 1993); Crawford Young, "The End of the Post-Colonial State in Africa? Reflections on Changing African Political Dimensions," *African Affairs* 103, no. 410 (2004): 23–49.

2   Mahmood Mamdani, *Citizen and Subject: Contemporary Africa and the Legacy of Late Colonialism* (Princeton, NJ: Princeton University Press, 1996), 16–18.

3   Mamdani, *Citizen and Subject*, 24.

4   Mamdani, *Citizen and Subject*, 16–18.

5   Mamdani, *Citizen and Subject,* 16–18.

6   Mamdani, *Citizen and Subject*, 287–8.

7   Mamdani, *Citizen and Subject*, 16–18.

8   Mamdani, *Citizen and Subject*, 296–7.

MODULE 6
SECONDARY IDEAS

KEY POINTS

- There are several subordinate ideas in *Citizen and Subject.* The three key issues Mamdani explores are the ways in which society in Africa is explained, how concepts of ethnicity* and the customary* are analyzed, and how there can be a new way of understanding direct and indirect colonial rule.

- Mamdani holds that ethnicity is a political idea, a structure invented to serve a purpose. That purpose is first to rule, and then to resist that rule.

- The impact of secondary ideas in *Citizen and Subject* has been limited, apart from the argument about ethnicity.

Other Ideas

Mahmood Mamdani develops several other arguments in *Citizen and Subject* that are not so much secondary ideas, as building blocks on which the book's main argument is constructed.

Citizen and Subject is also an investigation of debates and views about political economy* and civil society.* The political economy discourse is concerned with the connection between the mode of production and power.[1] Meanwhile, debates on civil society—those organizations that do not belong to the state but which are important in the make-up of society, such as churches and trade unions—are based on the idea that civil society in Africa is the same as civil society in Europe. These discourses also suppose that what drives democratization* is the tension between the state and that civil society.[2] These ways of looking at things are all based on models from European history.

> ❝ ... modern tribalism has to be understood not only as a historical phenomenon, but also as one that is contradictory. It signifies both the form of rule and the form of revolt against it. Whereas the former is oppressive, the latter may be emancipatory. ❞
>
> Mahmood Mamdani, *Citizen and Subject*

The rejection of these ways of thinking reflects Mamdani's rejection of history by analogy,* an important characteristic of his work.[3] As far as Mamdani is concerned, discussing Africa in the same terms as we discuss Europe, despite their very different histories, does not do justice to the historic reality of Africa.[4] *Citizen and Subject* focuses on historic experiences that are specific to the history of the African state. Mamdani also argues that South Africa's apartheid* rule was not that different from colonial rule. Looking at South Africa as an exception to the general historic experiences in Africa—what Mamdani calls exceptionalism—is a long-standing assumption in African Studies. It's an assumption that says South Africa's historic development differed so much from the rest of the continent that it has to be considered an exception.[5]

To develop his argument about the bifurcated state*—the division in both law and administration between rural and urban areas—Mamdani also provides an in-depth historic analysis of certain instrumental concepts of colonial rule. These concepts are customary,* tribalism,* and ethnicity. Mamdani discusses their relevance in the context of modern statehood and governance. Building on this, he argues that direct rule (favored by the French) and indirect rule* (via local authorities, and favored by the British) were not contradictory models of colonial* rule at all. In fact, they were complementary: together they formed rule in the bifurcated state. So Mamdani's analysis of the colonial state provides a new understanding of the nature of colonial rule.

Exploring the Ideas

Mamdani's deconstruction of the concepts of customary, tribalism, and ethnicity, and his rejection of South African exceptionalism* were ideas that had real impact among his peers.

South Africa is one of the two main case studies in *Citizen and Subject*. And it's on this case study that the arguments about the whole of sub-Saharan Africa are built. The choice of South Africa as a perfectly good example of the whole of Africa is unconventional. Generally, classifications such as sub-Saharan Africa or Black Africa did not include South Africa. The assumption is that South Africa's experience of apartheid rule was so different from the colonial experience in other African countries, that South Africa is an exception to continent-wide historical experiences rather than a typical example. Mamdani, however, argues that rather than the exception to the rule, the apartheid state was the quintessential realization of the bifurcated state, where white and urban areas were governed through direct rule, and rural and non-white areas through indirect rule. Mamdani's analysis of South Africa made its historic experience part of the historic experience of the rest of the continent.[6]

Mamdani's deconstruction of the concepts of the customary, ethnicity, and tribalism is also an important part of the bifurcated-state argument. He shows how traditional structures of governance were essential to colonial rural governance. For that reason, traditional structures should not be understood in isolation from the system of rule, because they are essential for understanding both colonial and postcolonial statehood* and governance in Africa. By deconstructing the structure of the customary, Mamdani shows how it has been invented and used by the colonial state to bolster colonial rule.[7] What was considered traditional and customary was often not very traditional at all. Yet in the postcolonial state, these so-called customary and traditional structures have continued to play a role in local governance.

Others share Mamdani's view that ethnicity and identity are not ancient and natural, but rather human constructions, which can be easily manipulated in the context of conflict, whether it be political or economic.[8] Mamdani shows how these concepts were given shape and meaning during the colonial era. He also shows how they became part of the system of colonial rule, and how they also play a role in the postcolonial state. His analysis has made a valuable contribution to our understanding of identity and ethnicity in the context of the modern African state.

Mamdani's analysis provides an important narrative of the origins of ethnicity and the customary and how they function in the interface between power and resistance in the modern state. Ethnicity is at one and the same time a structure of power and control, as well as a structure of resistance against this power.[9] What this means is that ethnicity became a structure through which African people were ruled and controlled in colonial times. But their resistance against this oppressive rule was also organized within these ethnic structures, as an identity group. So this resistance actually reproduced the structure of power it was itself resisting. Later in his career Mamdani would build further on these ideas that he first explores in *Citizen and Subject*.[10]

Overlooked

Citizen and Subject makes unstated connections with other theories of power, hegemony (the dominance of one state or social group over another), and resistance to power. *Citizen and Subject* argues that the way resistance to colonialism*—and then resistance to the postcolonial state—sprang up was shaped by the institutional framework of the colonial state itself. This relationship between dominant structures and resistance is not a new argument. Critical theorists* such as Michel Foucault* and Michel de Certeau* developed ideas that underlined the same connections between power and resistance to it.[11] The same ideas, meanwhile, have been outlined in the context of the non-Western world by authors like Homi K. Bhabha,* Edward Said,* Frantz Fanon,* and Gayatri Chakravorty Spivak.* They have argued to show how this resistance is complicit in the structures of power, because resistance can only work within the structures of power it seeks to resist. This is similar to Mamdani's argument about ethnicity as a structure of power and resistance.[12] Mamdani's work contributes to this debate, because it shows how the relationship between power and resistance carried on after the colonial era. He also demonstrates how Africans have since taken up these structures of power and resistance

NOTES

1   Iain McLean and Alistair McMillan, *Oxford Concise Dictionary of Politics* (Oxford: Oxford University Press, 2003), 418.

2   Rita Abrahamsen, *Disciplining Democracy: Development Discourse and Good Governance in Africa* (London: Zed Books, 2000), 52–4.

3   Mahmood Mamdani, *Citizen and Subject: Contemporary Africa and the Legacy of Late Colonialism* (Princeton, NJ: Princeton University Press, 1996), 9–10.

4   Mamdani, *Citizen and Subject*, 9–10.

5   Mamdani, Citizen and Subject, 27–8.

6   Mamdani, *Citizen and* Subject, 27.

7   Mamdani, *Citizen and Subject*, 111–28.

8   Mamdani, *Citizen and Subject*, 183–5.

9   Mamdani, *Citizen and Subject*, 183.

10 Mahmood Mamdani, *When Victims Become Killers: Colonialism, Nativism and the Genocide in Rwanda* (Oxford: James Currey, 2001); Mahmood Mamdani, *Define and Rule: Native as Political Identity* (Cambridge, MA: Harvard University Press, 2012).

11 Michel de Certeau, *The Practice of Everyday Life* (Berkeley: University of California Press, 1984); Michel Foucault, *Discipline and Punish: The Birth of the Prison* (London: Penguin, 1991); Ilan Kapoor, *The Postcolonial Politics of Development* (New York: Routledge, 2008).

12 Frantz Fanon, *The Wretched of the Earth* (London: Penguin, 1967); Edward W. Said, *Orientalism* (London: Penguin, 2003); Homi K. Bhabha, *The Location of Culture* (London: Routledge, 2008); Gayatri Chakravorty Spivak, "Can the Subaltern Speak?" in *Marxism and the Interpretation of Culture*, eds. Cary Nelson and Lawrence Grossberg (Urbana: University of Illinois Press, 1988), 271–313.

MODULE 7
ACHIEVEMENT

KEY POINTS

- With *Citizen and Subject*, Mamdani argues against the mainstream understanding of the crisis of the African state,* identifying it as a crisis rooted in the legacy of colonialism.*

- The most important factor in arriving at this conclusion is Mamdani's unique approach to the history of the African state's institutions.

- The fact that Mamdani's claims and arguments about the whole of sub-Saharan Africa are mainly based on the case studies of Uganda and South Africa do, however, limit his arguments.

Assessing the Argument

By writing *Citizen and Subject*, Mahmood Mamdani aimed to provide an understanding of the crisis of the African state in the late twentieth century that emphasized its historic roots. These roots are, according to Mamdani, located in the institutional legacy of colonialism.

The argument Mamdani makes is truly original. The wave of transitions to democracy seemed to show that African states had somehow overcome the legacy of colonialism. Mamdani, however, said the opposite was true. He argued that the failures of the democratization* processes in Africa were *caused* by the institutional legacy of colonialism, a legacy that was largely unrecognized. *Citizen and Subject* shows the link between colonialism and the contemporary challenges of the state and of governing in Africa. The focus on the institutional legacy left behind in the wake of the colonial experience, and sanctioned in law and governance, was new. It shifted attention

> ❝ *Citizen and Subject* is an impeccably clear treatise. Mamdani's arguments will be of interest to Africanists in various disciplines [...], and the arguments should invite a rethinking of some of the major notions relating to the colonial experience and its consequences for the state in Africa. ❞
>
> N. Ndegwa, review of *Citizen and Subject: Contemporary Africa and the Legacy of Late Colonialism*

from simply theorizing about state and governance in Africa to properly understanding political practices within African states' institutional framework.[1] This refocusing not only helped build an understanding of problems, but also clearly pointed towards solutions.[2]

Achievement in Context

Citizen and Subject appeared at a time when people were looking for solutions to important issues. When the book was published in 1996, Africa had just experienced a wave of democratic transitions, but initial optimism about the future was waning.[3] Concerns about the state of democracy in Africa, and how best to contribute to democratization processes, have remained important to policy makers ever since.[4] In the 1990s, both scholars and those involved in democratization initiatives focused their attention on civil society* as the best way to pursue goals of democratization and good governance.* They were convinced that poor and untrustworthy political culture and political practices were the main obstacles to achieving the good governance and democracy people hoped for. Mamdani thought otherwise. He argued that the inherited institutional set up of the contemporary African state was the main obstacle to progress. Mamdani's focus on this important theme meant *Citizen and Subject* reached a wide and varied audience. What has made the book stand out is its unique historic-institutional* approach to the crisis of statehood in Africa. Because it provides a general approach to understanding both the historic and the institutional roots of current challenges, *Citizen and Subject* has remained important for everybody who wants to understand state and governance in Africa.

Limitations

Citizen and Subject focuses on Africa and the crisis of governance in the African state during the late twentieth century. Although Mamdani's analyses could be valuable for comparative studies of colonialism across the globe, his text deals specifically with Africa's colonial and postcolonial experience, so its relevance is limited to Africa. The book has been criticized for making generalizations about African colonial and postcolonial history, because it is mainly based on just two case studies of Uganda and South Africa.[5] It is fair to say that *Citizen and Subject* is particularly relevant for the study of South Africa and Uganda, while it provides a general argument about the postcolonial African state of the rest of Africa. Mamdani's argument applies to other states to a greater or lesser extent, depending on the individual case. And because it focuses only on late twentieth-century Africa, the book's scope is also limited in terms of its timescale.

It's also true that *Citizen and Subject* doesn't bring much to the debate about economy that has emerged since the book was published. Since the late 1990s, Africa has experienced an economic boom, leading some to argue that the twenty-first century will be dominated economically by Africa.[6] This economic boom is not only limited to countries that have oil and other useful resources—even countries that are in conflict are experiencing impressive growth rates in an era of overall global economic crisis.[7] Yet critics suggest the economic boom has brought even greater inequality, something that will undermine governments, institutions, and markets in the long run.[8] According to others, the nature of the economic growth in Africa has, from an international economic point of view, deepened Africa's globally dependent position.[9] This contemporary debate is mainly about Africa's economic growth and its effects, but it also touches on wider questions of economic and political liberalization and democratization in Africa. Mamdani's argument says little about this ongoing academic debate on economic and political change in Africa.

NOTES

1   Martin Murray, "Configuring the trajectory of African political history," *Canadian Journal of Contemporary African Studies* 34, no. 2 (2000): 386.

2   Adam Leach, "Review of *Citizen and Subject*," *Review of African Political Economy* 24, no. 72 (1997): 297.

3   Crawford Young, "The Third Wave of Democratization in Africa: Ambiguities and Contradictions," in *State, Conflict and Democracy,* ed. Richard Joseph (Boulder, CO: Lynne Rienner, 1999), 25.

4   Gabrielle Lynch and Gordon Crawford, "Democratization in Africa 1990–2010: An Assessment," *Democratization* 18, no. 2 (2011): 275–310.

5   John A. Wiseman, "Review of *Citizen and Subject*," *Journal of Developing Areas* 31, no. 2 (1997): 274.

6   Charles Robertson et al., *The Fastest Billion: the Story Behind Africa's Economic Revolution* (London: Renaissance Capital, 2012).

7   Shantayanan Devarajan and Wolfgang Fengler, "Africa's Economic Boom: Why the Pessimists and the Optimists Are Both Right," *Foreign Affairs* (May/June 2013).

8   Africa Progress Panel, *Jobs, Justice and Equity: Seizing Opportunities in Times of Global Change. Africa Progress Report 2012* (Africa Progress Panel, 2012), 8.

9   Ian Taylor, *Africa Rising? BRICS – Diversifying Dependency* (London: James Currey, 2014), 3.

MODULE 8
PLACE IN THE AUTHOR'S WORK

KEY POINTS

- Mamdani is an Africanist. His work focuses on governance, conflict, identity, and citizenship in Africa.

- *Citizen and Subject* was the text in which Mamdani first developed ideas and concepts he would further explore in his subsequent work.

- *Citizen and Subject* is Mamdani's most famous work, and it established his international reputation and career.

Positioning

When *Citizen and Subject* was first published in 1996, Mamdani was 50, and had just started a professorship at the University of Cape Town in South Africa. The book builds on his earlier work on social movements, agriculture, and development in rural Uganda and his research on methods of native control in apartheid* South Africa.[1] Mamdani also touches on core themes of *Citizen and Subject* in some of his earlier work, such as *Politics and Class Formation in Uganda* .[2] In this work, Mamdani analyses the politics of class, race, and tribes in modern Uganda and argues that both the colonial* and postcolonial state* have played a part in the formation of the class system there. According to Mamdani, colonial rule "reduced all contradictions between classes within the colony to secondary significance."[3] However, after independence, a class struggle emerged between a domestic bourgeois elite and an economic underclass.[4] The impact of colonialism* on political identities and struggles is developed in *Citizen and Subject*.

Not long after the publication of *Citizen and Subject,* Mamdani became the President of CODESRIA,* the Council for the

> **"** By politicizing indigeneity,* the colonial state set
> in motion a process with the potential of endlessly
> spawning identities animated by the distinctions
> indigenous and nonindigenous, and polarizing them.
> This indeed set the context in which political violence
> unfolded in Africa, colonial as well as postcolonial. **"**
>
> Mahmood Mamdani, *When Victims Become Killers*

Development of Social Science Research in Africa. This was a prestigious position that he held from 1998 to 2002. During this period, Mamdani started to focus more directly on contemporary conflict in Africa. In 1997, he was part of a CODESRIA mission to the Kivu region in the eastern part of the Democratic Republic of Congo. He presented his findings on the root causes of the violence being experienced there to the CODESRIA general assembly.[5] Continuing his research on the crisis in the Great Lakes region,* Mamdani published *When Victims Become Killers* in 2001.[6] By that time, he had already moved from the University of Cape Town to the University of Columbia, New York, where he continued to research conflict in Africa. Mamdani is currently Herbert Lehman Professor of Government in the department of anthropology and political science and the School of International and Public Affairs at Columbia University, as well as director of the Makerere Institute of Social Research, in Kampala, Uganda. In 2008, Mamdani was voted ninth top public intellectual by *Prospect Magazine* and *Foreign Policy*.[7]

Integration

Citizen and Subject builds on Mamdani's earlier work, and although he had used political economy* as the framework for *Politics and Class Formation in Uganda,* he nevertheless totally rejects it as an analytical framework in *Citizen and Subject*. Political economy analysis focuses on the connection between the mode of production—that is the way an economy is set up—and the nature of power. In *Citizen and Subject*, however, Mamdani abandons this approach and argues that modes of production cannot explain the history of the postcolonial African state very well. Having started his work on the book from a political economy perspective, Mamdani was not satisfied with where this line of enquiry was leading him. He eventually concluded that the state that had developed in postcolonial Africa was not dependent on the mode of production. Rather, it was shaped by the "the native question instead of the labor question."[8] This is why *Citizen and Subject* marked a shift in Mamdani's work. After *Citizen and Subject*, he would focus particularly on conflict, citizenship, identity, and ethnicity* as political identity in the context of the modern state. The ideas developed in *Citizen and Subject* offered Mamdani the foundations for his highly praised research on the Rwandan genocide,* the Great Lakes region of Africa, and the conflict in Darfur.*[9]

Significance

Citizen and Subject was a turning point in Mamdani's career. The publication of the book established his reputation as a critical scholar of governance and conflict in contemporary Africa, and as someone who often defends provocative views. As well as laying the theoretical foundations for his later work, *Citizen and Subject* won the prestigious African Studies Association Herskovits Prize for the most important scholarly work in 1997.[10] In the years following the publication of *Citizen and Subject*, Mamdani would grow as an influential African scholar on themes of conflict in Africa, identity and conflict, and governance and conflict, and he has published many important analyses of conflict. Insights into the roots of these conflicts go back to the arguments Mamdani set out in *Citizen and Subject*; as such this book was essential for the development of later case studies. He continues to participate actively in public and academic debate on conflicts in Africa, most notably in the case of the conflict in the Darfur* region of Sudan, where he criticized activists for misrepresenting the crisis to follow their own interests.[11]

NOTES

1   Mamdani, *Citizen and Subject: Contemporary Africa and the Legacy of Late Colonialism* (Princeton, NJ: Princeton University Press, 1996), ix; Mahmood Mamdani, "Analysing the Agrarian Question: the Case of a Buganda Village," *Mawazo* 5, no. 3 (1983): 47–64; Mahmood Mamdani, "Forms of Labour an Accumulation of Capital: Analysis of a Village in Lango, Northern Uganda," *Mawazo* 5, no. 4 (1983): 44–65; Mahmood Mamdani, "Extreme But Not Exceptional: Towards an Analysis of the Agrarian Question in Uganda," *Journal of Peasant Studies* 14, no. 2 (1987): 191–225; Mahmood Mamdani, *African Studies in Social Movements and Democracy* (Dakar: CODESRIA, 1995).

2   Mahmood Mamdani, *Politics and Class Formation in Uganda* (London: Heinemann Educational, 1976).

3   Mamdani, *Politics and Class Formation*, 221.

4   Mamdani, *Politics and Class Formation*, 313.

5   Mahmood Mamdani, *Understanding the Crisis in Kivu: Report of the CODESRIA Mission to the Democratic Republic of Congo, September 1997* (Dakar: CODESRIA).

6   See Mahmood Mamdani, *When Victims Become Killers: Colonialism, Nativism and the Genocide in Rwanda* (Oxford: James Currey, 2001).

7   Anonymous, "The World's Top 20 Public Intellectuals," *Foreign Policy* 167 (2008), 54–7.

8   Mamdani, *Citizen and Subject*, 23.

9   See Mamdani, *When Victims Become Killers and Mahmood Mamdani, Saviours and Survivors: Darfur, Politics, and the War on Terror* (Cape Town: Human Sciences Research Council, 2009).

10 "J. Melville Herskovits Award," African Studies Association, accessed January 2, 2015, http://www.africanstudies.org/awards-prizes/herskovits-award.

11 Mahmood Mamdani, "Prof. Mahmood Mamdani and John Prendergast, The Darfur Debate," April 14, 2009, [19:17–19:35], accessed January 11, 2015, https://www.youtube.com/watch?v=yGOpfH_5_pY.

SECTION 3
IMPACT

MODULE 9
THE FIRST RESPONSES

KEY POINTS

- *Citizen and Subject* has been criticized for drawing overly generalized conclusions based on just two case studies. Critics have also said the work ignores the diversity of the continent, as well as historic processes that don't fit the analytical framework.

- There has been little direct response by Mamdani to his scholarly critics. Where he has responded, he has defended his arguments, particularly using Africa as a unit of analysis, even though this results in generalized arguments.

- Mamdani continues to place identity, ethnicity,* and colonial legacies at the center of contemporary conflict in Africa, though he now avoids arguments that span the entire continent.

Criticism

When Mahmood Mamdani first published *Citizen and Subject* in 1996, it immediately received a lot of attention in scholarly journals in a number of different disciplines,[1] and has since been recognized as an important contribution to African scholarly literature. But despite this positive reception, *Citizen and Subject* has also been criticized. The second part of the book, "The Anatomy of Resistance," received the strongest criticism, mainly for drawing conclusions that some critics said were too generalized, being based on case material from only two countries, Uganda and South Africa.

It is not surprising that *Citizen and Subject* has been criticized for being too generalized,[2] for making sweeping claims,[3] and for ignoring

55

> 66 ... this type of historical approach is debatable because the historical unity of Black Africa is a colonial chimera. Social history in the last 15 years has tried to draw another picture, more detailed, more empirical but also better documented, of local and global interactions. 99
>
> Jean Copans, "Review"

the diversity of different countries' colonial and postcolonial histories.[4] After all, the book looks at broad themes and takes a whole continent as a unit of analysis.[5] However, the book should be read as a general theoretical argument that case-specific studies will then spring from.

Citizen and Subject has been examined by various academic disciplines beyond its own specialist field of the African state* and governance. These disciplines include history, ethnography,* development, sociology, and peace studies.[6] It is worth noting that historians criticized Mamdani's work much more than scholars in the social sciences and in the specialist field of state and governance in Africa.[7] Although *Citizen and Subject* never set out to be a work of African history,[8] it has nonetheless been hailed as an important contribution to African historical writing by several leading scholars of African history[9] and journals that cover the same subject. It has often been considered as a work of African historiography.*[10] But historians have almost unanimously criticized *Citizen and Subject* for lacking nuance, for not being rigorous enough, for ignoring historic process where it did not fit the author's framework, and for historical inaccuracies.[11]

Responses

Mamdani did not generally respond to reviews of *Citizen and Subject*, nor to the criticism or praise he received. One notable exception, however, is a response to a review by the French anthropologist and sociologist Jean Copans.*[12] Copans argued that: "Mamdani's insights are usually to the point but *Citizen and Subject* is a book of one and only one idea: African history is best explained by the gap between rural and urban and the best example of this colonial outcome is South Africa, typical rather than exceptional. This is a very schematic interpretation of the past and present of the continent: all the works of anthropology, history, political science that I have read in the last 15 years try to overcome this Western (and colonial) prejudice! […] This book does not do justice to the specific complexities of Black Africa."[13]

In his response, Mamdani begins by stating that his book is not a piece of African history, but a historically informed look at the contemporary African state.[14] Because *Citizen and Subject* was well received, yet was also heavily criticized by historians, Mamdani felt the need to clarify "lest readers […] are led into thinking that the book under discussion is a work of history."[15] Although Mamdani agrees with some of the nuances Copans highlights, he defends his decision to use all of Africa as a unit of analysis. He claims it is a meaningful way to understand political dynamics on the African continent, despite the consequential generalizations.[16]

The journal *African Sociological Review* published a symposium, or convention, on *Citizen and Subject*, where it was reviewed by several scholars.[17] Mamdani decided to respond to these scholars, leading to an interesting and rare case of a direct discussion between an author and his critics in a journal. The debate showed just how important *Citizen and Subject* is. The discussion about Mamdani's use of the concepts of ethnicity and customary* in this review symposium is very interesting. For example, one of the reviewers criticizes Mamdani for using the concept of ethnicity in the context of peasant revolt.[18] Mamdani responds by stating, at length, that the use of the concept of ethnicity is not about ethnicity as such. Rather, he says, it is about ethnicity as politically enforced by customary power in the colonial state. Mamdani is also keen to emphasize that for him, the customary is where the battle is taking place. It is neither "a cultural residue," something left over from colonial times, as one of the reviewers suggests, nor "a pure invention."[19]

Conflict and Consensus

Criticisms of *Citizen and Subject* have not led Mamdani to revise any of his arguments in the book, nor to rethink any of his ideas. The critique and Mamdani's responses to it should be understood as ongoing academic debate, and this is common in academia. The themes of citizenship, ethnicity, identity, and conflict continue to be topical in African Studies, and Mamdani's *Citizen and Subject* is now established as a seminal work as these themes continue to be debated. However this does not mean that individual scholars working on these themes no longer contest his arguments. In his later publications on conflict in the Great Lakes region,* Darfur,* and the War on Terror,* Mamdani continues to place identity, ethnicity, and colonial legacies at the center of contemporary conflict in Africa. Interestingly, though, in these works he takes a more case-oriented approach, instead of trying to develop continent-wide arguments.[20]

NOTES

1   For example, Franz Ansprenger, "Review of *Citizen and Subject*," The *International Journal of African Historical Studies* 30, no. 3 (1997): 719–20; Frederick Cooper, "Review of *Citizen and Subject*," *International Labor and Working Class History* 52 (1997): 156–60; Gail M. Gerhart, "Review of *Citizen and Subject*," *Foreign Affairs* 76, no. 2 (1997): 199–200; Jeffrey Herbst, "Review of *Citizen and Subject*," *Annals of the American Academy of Political and Social Science* 554 (1997): 216–17; Preben Kaarsholm, "Review of *Citizen and Subject*," *Journal of Southern African Studies* 23, no. 2 (1997): 386–8; Adam Leach, "Review of *Citizen and Subject*," *Review of African Political Economy* 24, no. 72 (1997): 295–7; John Lonsdale, "Review of *Citizen and Subject*," *Journal of African History* 38, no. 3 (1997): 520–2; Knut Nustad, "Review of *Citizen and Subject*," *Journal of Peace Research* 35, no. 5 (1998): 650; Carolyn Martin Shaw, "Review of *Citizen and Subject*," *American Ethnologist* 25, no. 3 (1998): 531–2; John A. Wiseman, "Review of *Citizen and Subject*," *Journal of Developing Areas* 31,

no. 2 (1997): 273–5.

2   Wiseman, "Review," 74.

3   Jean Copans, "Review of *Citizen and Subject*," *Transformation* 36 (1998): 102–5; Pierre Englebert, "The Contemporary African State: Neither African nor State," *Third World Quarterly* 18, no. 4 (1997): 774; Martin Murray, "Configuring the Trajectory of African Political History," *Canadian Journal of African Studies* 34, no. 2 (2000): 376–86.

4   Copans, "Review," 102–5; Englebert, "The Contemporary African State," 774; Murray, "Configuring the Trajectory," 376–86.

5   Mahmood Mamdani, *Citizen and Subject: Contemporary Africa and the Legacy of Late Colonialism* (Princeton, NJ: Princeton University Press, 1996), 8.

6   Ansprenger, "Review," 719–20; Cooper, "Review," 156–60; Stuart Douglas, "Review of *Citizen and Subject*," *American Anthropologist* 100, no. 2 (1998): 550–1; Englebert, "The Contemporary African State," 767–75; Edmund Harsch, "African States in Social and Historical Context," *Sociological Forum* 12, no. 4 (1997): 671–9; Leach, "Review of *Citizen and Subject*," *Development in Practice* 7, no. 3 (1997): 314–15; Lonsdale, "Review," 520–2; Shaw, "Review," 531–2; Nustad, "Review," 650; Tignor, "Review," 1541; Wiseman, "Review;" Eric Msinde Aseka et al., "Review Symposium: Mahmood Mamdani and the Analysis of African Society," *African Sociological Review* 1, no. 2 (1997): 96–144

7   Herbst, "Review," 216–17; Englebert, "The Contemporary African State," 767–75; Tom Young, "Review Article: The State and Politics in Africa," *Journal of Southern African Studies* 25, no. 1 (1999): 149–54; Ian S. Spears, "Review of *After Colnialism* and *Citizen and Subject*," *Canadian Jounrla of African Studies* 30, no. 1 (1997): 177–9.

8   Mahmood Mamdani, "Commentary: Mahmood Mamdani Responds to Jean Copans' Review in *Transformation* 36," *Transformation* 39 (1999): 97–101.

9   Cooper, "Review," 156–60; Lonsdale, "Review."

10 Lonsdale, "Review," 520–2; Cooper, "Review," 156–60; P. L. E. Idahosa, "Review of *Citizen and Subject*," *International History Review* 20, no. 2 (1998): 493–6; Ralph A. Austen, "Review of *Citizen and Subject*," *Law and History Review* 17, no. 2 (1999): 406–8.

11 Austen, "Review;" Cooper, "Review;" Lonsdale, "Review;" Chris Youé, "Mamdani's History," *Canadian Journal of African Studies* 34, no. 2 (2000): 397–408.

12 Mamdani, "Commentary;" Copans, "Review," 102–5.

13 Copans, "Review," 104–5

14 Mamdani, "Commentary," 97.

15 Mamdani, "Commentary," 97.

16 Mamdani, "Commentary," 100–1.

17 Mahmood Mamdani, "A Response to Comments," *African Sociological Review* 1, no. 2 (1997): 145–55; Eric Msinde Aseka et al., "Review Symposium: Mahmood Mamdani and the Analysis of African Society," *African Sociological Review* 1, no. 2 (1997): 96–144.

18 Ran Greenstein, "Review of *Citizen and Subject*," *African Sociological Review* 1, no. 2 (1997): 111–15.

19 Mamdani, "Commentary," 148.

20 Mahmood Mamdani, *When Victims Become Killers: Colonialism, Nativism and the Genocide in Rwanda* (Oxford: James Currey, 2001); Mahmood Mamdani, *Good Muslim, Bad Muslim: America, the Cold War, and the Roots of Terror* (New York: Pantheon Books, 2004); Mahmood Mamdani, *Saviours and Survivors: Darfur, Politics, and the War on Terror* (Cape Town: Human Sciences Research Council, 2009).

MODULE 10
THE EVOLVING DEBATE

KEY POINTS

- Mamdani's arguments about identity, conflict, and citizenship in the postcolonial African state* have been important in the public debate on these topics. Indeed, Mamdani himself has actively participated in these debates.

- *Citizen and Subject* has inspired historians, political scientists, lawyers, and many others interested in the problems of the contemporary African state, but has not been central to the formation of an identifiable school of thought.

- *Citizen and Subject* remains an important text for Africanists interested in postcolonial history, conflict, identity, governance, and the crisis of the state in Africa.

Uses and Problems

Mahmood Mamdani is an active academic and has built on the ideas of *Citizen and Subject: Contemporary Africa and the Legacy of Late Colonialism*. The book was to be the foundation for Mamdani's further work, yet whereas he draws on two cases in *Citizen and Subject*—Uganda and South Africa—to make general arguments about the postcolonial African state, the work that followed would be rooted in specific case studies.

Mamdani has published on the Rwandan genocide* and the crisis in the Great Lakes region* afterwards. In *When Victims Become Killers: Colonialism, Nativism, and the Genocide in Rwanda*, Mamdani puts ethnicity* and identity center stage as a political construct* originating in the colonial era. He goes on to examine how the politicization of

> **❝** Americans think Darfur is a tragic genocide.
> Mamdani thinks the reality is more complex. His ideas
> should be taken seriously for a number of reasons,
> especially because he provides a road map to a workable
> peace settlement. **❞**
>
> Joel Whitney, "The Genocide Myth," in *Guernica* online magazine
> (guernicamag.com)

ethnicity and identity has contributed to cycles of violence and genocide in Rwanda since its independence.[1]

In his next publication, 2004's *Good Muslim, Bad Muslim: America, the Cold War, and the Roots of Terror*, Mamdani also focuses on questions of identity and the role of foreign political interests. *Good Muslim, Bad Muslim* is a non-Western look at the Cold War* and the rise of terrorism.[2] Mamdani writes a historical analysis that criticizes the use of history by analogy,* just as he did in *Citizen and Subject*. He also builds on the argument he put forward in *Citizen and Subject* that conflicts in Africa have their roots in Western policy on Africa and governance of Africans. The War on Terror* is a contemporary discourse that has an impact on how Africa and African conflicts are understood.

Mamdani has also published material on the crisis in Darfur,* where he elaborates his arguments about Western policy and conflict in Africa. In *Saviours and Survivors: Darfur, Politics, and the War on Terror*, he talks about the crisis in Darfur in the context of Western foreign policy that has misrepresented the conflict there in terms of the War on Terror.[3] In *Saviours and Survivors*, as in his most recent publication, *Define and Rule: Native as Political Identity,*[4] Mamdani uses another of the core themes of *Citizen and Subject*—the construction of identity and its roots—as central for understanding contemporary conflict and terrorism.

These published works fall into the disciplinary fields of contemporary conflict in Africa, identity, and citizenship, but they inform the field of international relations. The later books do not challenge or change Mamdani's earlier arguments, but instead develop his main ideas and themes. They deal with cases that are relevant beyond academia and beyond African Studies as well, mainly because they are linked to Western foreign policy. This means they have received a lot of attention in the media, much more than *Citizen and Subject* did when it was published.

Schools of Thought

Citizen and Subject is an influential text in African Studies. It has inspired historians, political scientists, lawyers, and many other people interested in the problems of the contemporary African state. The book has not been central in the formation of an identifiable school of thought, but it has made an important contribution to African Studies. It has challenged mainstream approaches to the crisis of the African state and offered an understanding of contemporary challenges in Africa based on its own history. It is an important book for students in the curriculum of contemporary African Studies, particularly for students of African politics, governance, and postcolonial history. In textbooks on African politics, Mamdani's argument about decentralized despotism* as a system of colonial and postcolonial rule is used to explain the contemporary problems of the African state and the paradoxes that can be seen in the practice of politics in Africa.[5] Historian Frederick Cooper* uses Mamdani's argument about the understanding of the tribe as an institution of authority to explain the rise of ethnic politics in post–apartheid* South Africa. He not only uses Mamdani's meaning of tribe, but also his argument that these concepts apply to South Africa just as much as to any other African country.

In Current Scholarship

Although *Citizen and Subject* has gained a prominent place in current scholarship, not everybody agrees with Mamdani's arguments. In his book on politics in contemporary Africa, Africanist Patrick Chabal* agrees with Mamdani that colonialism* has institutionalized both citizen and subject as political identities. But he goes on to insist that this does not necessarily reflect political identities in the way Africans themselves have experienced them. According to Chabal, these categories of citizen and subject are not fixed. They are fluid, partly overlapping, and even merging at times, while people constantly straddle citizenship and subjecthood in different contexts.[6] American political scientist Jeffrey Herbst* was interested in Mamdani's argument of decentralized despotism as a structure of local governance that emerged during the colonial era and continues to exist in postcolonial Africa. He thought it offered an important contribution to his study of the practices of authority and control in postcolonial Africa. For Herbst, the main problem of establishing effective governance in Africa lies in states' ability to effectively "broadcast" their power over the whole territory. Mamdani's decentralized despotism offers an understanding of the historical roots of the challenges of establishing effective governance over rural areas.[7] In short, his work is often cited as a point of reference on which scholars continue to build their research and analyses of contemporary African politics and governance.

NOTES

1   Mahmood Mamdani, *When Victims Become Killers: Colonialism, Nativism and the Genocide in Rwanda* (Oxford: James Currey, 2001).

2   Mahmood Mamdani, *Good Muslim, Bad Muslim: America, the Cold War, and the Roots of Terror* (New York: Pantheon Books, 2004).

3   Mahmood Mamdani, *Saviours and Survivors: Darfur, Politics, and the War on Terror* (Cape Town: Human Sciences Research Council, 2009).

4   Mahmood Mamdani, *Define and Rule: Native as Political Identity* (Cambridge, MA: Harvard University Press, 2012).

5   Pierre Englebert and Kevin C. Dunn, *Inside African Politics* (Boulder, CO: Lynne Rienner, 2013), 30, 60; Goran Hyden, *African Politics in Comparative Perspective* (Cambridge: Cambridge University Press, 2006), 53.

6   Patrick Chabal, *Africa: The Politics of Suffering and Smiling* (London: Zed Books, 2009), 89, 103.

7   Jeffrey Herbst, *States and Power in Africa: Comparative Lessons in Authority and Control* (Princeton, NJ: Princeton University Press, 2009), 60–1.

MODULE 11
IMPACT AND INFLUENCE TODAY

KEY POINTS

- Because of Africa's ongoing challenges of state failure,* conflict, and processes of democratization,* *Citizen and Subject* continues to be an important text that offers an understanding of the historic roots of Africa's current situation.

- Both policy makers and a broader audience continue to appreciate these challenges, yet without taking the history of ethnic identity since the colonial period into consideration.

- In his subsequent work and in public debate on ongoing conflict in Africa, Mamdani argues that ethnicity* and identity are political constructs* and are themselves part of the structures of power, domination, and conflict.

Position

The arguments that Mahmood Mamdani developed in *Citizen and Subject*—arguments about citizenship, political identity, and the understanding of ethnicity as a political construct—are now even more relevant in the context of both academic and policy debates than when the book was published. In the years following the publication of *Citizen and Subject*, the scholarly debate about Africa's issues, the crisis of the state, governance failures, and the difficult transition to democracy have become dominated by the idea of state failure.* When Mamdani published *Citizen and Subject* in 1996, the concept of state failure was already in use, but it was not as widely used in the debate about the African state* as it would come to be in the following years. What Mamdani referred to as the African impasse* became

> ❝ ... part of being a 'public intellectual' is also having a talent for communicating with a wide and diverse public. ❞
>
> *Foreign Policy*, "The World's Top 20 Public Intellectuals."

framed as "state failure" after the late 1990s. This was generally summed up as a crisis of state and governance, declining economies, growing insecurity, and the eruption of violent conflict across the continent, as well as the erosion of the legitimacy of the state.[1]

The concept of state failure didn't just dominate the scholarly debate about the crisis of the African state and governance system. It also linked the problems of the state and governance system with violent conflict, civil war, and ethnic conflict. In the mid-1990s and early 2000s, many African countries were experiencing violent conflict. These conflicts were generally explained by this notion of state failure, which argued that existing social or ethnic tensions could easily turn into violent conflict when the state was falling apart.

The ideas in *Citizen and Subject* have been important in this debate, mainly because Mamdani continued to work on these themes himself.[2] Although *Citizen and Subject* aimed to shed light on the African impasse, its main contribution to the academic debate today lies elsewhere. It offers a theoretical and historically informed understanding of complex concepts such as the construction of ethnicity as a political identity. But it also outlines an understanding of citizenship in the modern African state in the context of contemporary conflict.

Interaction

In *Citizen and Subject*, Mamdani argues that to understand contemporary conflict in Africa you need to understand the history of ethnic identity and identity politics since the colonial period. These arguments confront the predominant ideas of foreign— meaning US or Western—policy makers, as well as those of influential advocacy groups, who work to support a particular cause. For example, the advocacy group "Save Darfur"* explained the conflict in Darfur* in terms of "race"—Arabs against Africans—and the War on Terror.* In the same vein, the Rwandan genocide* and the conflict in the Great Lakes region* are discussed in terms of ethnic primordialism.* Those who believe in ethnic primordialism are persuaded that ethnicities are a natural, ancient phenomenon. This is in contrast to those who see ethnicity as a social or political invention. Because these ways of explaining events have made the situation easier to understand for Western audiences and have played on both foreign policy and media interests in subjects such as genocide and terrorism, for example, these narratives have become influential in both public and policy debates, and to the community of people who support advocacy groups financially.

Mamdani's own work after *Citizen and Subject* focused on ethnicity as a political construct. Because these issues were part of both policy and public debate, Mamdani's arguments gained more exposure in the press than they did when he had first published his ideas in *Citizen and Subject*. Since the late 1990s, Mamdani has actively participated in debates in the media, discussing his arguments of ethnicity as a political construct dating back to the colonial period, and how ethnic identities have become polarized and politicized in the context of conflicts in Rwanda, the Great Lakes region, or Darfur.

The Continuing Debate

After publishing *Saviours and Survivors* in 2009, Mamdani has been part of the public debate about the Darfur crisis. Although this debate was directly linked to *Saviours and Survivors*, Mamdani's understanding of the conflict in Darfur builds directly on the ideas he first developed in *Citizen and Subject*. This means the public response to Mamdani's arguments about the Darfur conflict indirectly relates to *Citizen and Subject* as well. Mamdani gave interviews about the Darfur crisis and argued that the crisis was misrepresented by US policy makers and activist organizations as a conflict about race and terrorism.[3]

April 2009 saw what became known as "The Darfur Debate." Organized by Columbia University, this debate was between Mamdani and human rights activist and director of Enough Project* John Prendergast.* The debate focused on trying to understand the causes and nature of the conflict in Darfur and on identifying ways to bring an end to violence and to promote a sustainable peace. Mamdani argued that the root causes of contemporary violence in Darfur went back to the colonial era and specific structures of governance set up at the time.[4] He also argued that our understanding of the Darfur crisis was largely shaped by a "domestic movement" in the United States that had hugely inflated the numbers of deaths in the conflict. Mamdani said this domestic movement drove not only our understanding of the Darfur crisis, but also policy making in the United States.[5]

Although Prendergast agreed on the historic roots of the conflict, he maintained that the current crisis was different from the historic pattern of violence in the region. For him, the crisis in Darfur was the consequence of "maldevelopment, marginalization, an overconcentration of power in the center and the willingness to use any means necessary to maintain that power." Prendergast said these issues had not been addressed by external actors and, until they *were* addressed, conflict would continue in Sudan.[6]

The discussion between Prendergast and Mamdani shows that Mamdani is pursuing an academic argument, while Prendergast is interested in more concrete actions and policy making. Prendergast advocates using instruments of international law as well as holding people responsible for atrocities to account. Mamdani suggests that there are root causes to the problems, but does not define concrete responses to address the root causes. He believes that addressing the problems Prendergast outlines will not solve the structural concerns that go back to the colonial era. Providing humanitarian aid and applying international law is not the real challenge for him. The fundamental issue lies at the level of citizenship, of the definition and meaning given to citizenship and Mamdani thinks this has to be an internal process that cannot be driven by outside actors.[7]

NOTES

1   Robert I. Rotberg, "The Failure and Collapse of Nation-States: Breakdown, Prevention, and Repair," in *When States Fail: Causes and Consequences*, ed. Robert I. Rotberg (Princeton, NJ: Princeton University Press, 2004), 47.

2   Mahmood Mamdani, *When Victims Become Killers: Colonialism, Nativism and the Genocide in Rwanda* (Oxford: James Currey, 2001); Gerard Prunier, *The Rwanda Crisis: History of a Genocide* (London: Hurst, 1997).

3   See for example: Warscapes, "In Conversation with Mahmood Mamdani, by Bakhti Bhakti Shringarpure, July 15, 2013," accessed February 16, 2015, http://www.warscapes.com/conversations/conversation-mahmood-mamdani; Joel Whitney, "The Genocide Myth: Joel Whitney Interviews Mahmood Mamdani, May 12, 2009," accessed February 16, 2015, https://www.guernicamag.com/interviews/the_genocide_myth; Democracy Now!, "Mahmood Mamdani on Darfur: The Politics of Naming: Genocide, Civil War, Insurgency," accessed February 16, 2015, http://www.democracynow.org/2007/6/4/mahmood_mamdani_on_darfur_the_politics; Charlie Kimber, "Interview: Mahmood Mamdani on Darfur," *Socialist Review* 337 (2009).

4   Mahmood Mamdani, "Prof. Mahmood Mamdani and John Prendergast, 'The Darfur Debate'," April 14, 2009, [25:14–25:39], accessed January 11, 2015, https://www.youtube.com/watch?v=yGOpfH_5_pY.

5   Mamdani, "The Darfur Debate," 19:17–19:35.

6   John Prendergast, "Prof. Mahmood Mamdani and John Prendergast, 'The Darfur Debate'," April 14, 2009, [16:20–17:02], accessed January 11, 2015, https://www.youtube.com/watch?v=yGOpfH_5_pY.

7   Mamdani, "The Darfur Debate," 1:33:45–1:33:58.

WHERE NEXT?

KEY POINTS

- *Citizen and Subject* will likely remain an important text that links the legacy of colonialism* with challenges of conflict and governance in contemporary Africa.

- *Citizen and Subject* can be the basis for future scholarly arguments concerned with good governance* and democratization* in Africa.

- Scholars of contemporary Africa will continue to consider the book a seminal work, because it provides a historic narrative of the modern African state* and its sociopolitical structures.

Potential

As a challenge to mainstream ideas, Mahmood Mamdani's *Citizen and Subject: Contemporary Africa and the Legacy of Late Colonialism* is likely to remain an important contribution to the understanding of the current crisis of state and governance in Africa. The African impasse* that Mamdani aimed to understand when he first published the book in 1996 has since evolved. In the intervening years, some African countries have successfully democratized, while many others have experienced relapses into authoritarianism, civil conflicts, and state failure.*

The structural problems of state and governance failure that Mamdani addresses are still very present. These realities on the African continent make it likely that *Citizen and Subject* will continue to be an important work for scholars and policy makers interested in the crisis of the African state.

Mamdani argues that the colonial legacy of the contemporary African state is a key factor in understanding the challenges it faces today,

> ❝ *Citizen and Subject* will be required reading for Africanists. ❞
>
> Jeffrey Herbst, "Review of *Citizen and Subject*."

including political violence and ethnic conflict. He argues that, "If we are to make political violence thinkable, we need to understand the process by which victims and perpetrators become polarized as *group identities*. Who do perpetrators of violence think they are? And who do they think they will eliminate through violence? Even if the identities propelled through violence are drawn from outside the domain of politics—such as race (from biology) or ethnicity or religion (from culture)—we need to denaturalize these identities by outlining their history and illuminating their links with organized forms of power."[1]

Citizen and Subject is likely to remain a key reference for scholars of contemporary conflict and governance in Africa. It is a reminder of the historic roots of contemporary challenges and offers a way in which those challenges can be explored. Although Mamdani has insisted on several occasions that *Citizen and Subject* is not a work of African history, it is still likely that authors of late twentieth-century African history will continue to consider the book a seminal work, because it provides a history of the modern African state and its sociopolitical structures. For this reason—and despite the criticism of Mamdani's historic analysis—*Citizen and Subject* is likely to remain influential.

Future Directions

Mamdani is an active academic, and so is the foremost scholar pursuing the ideas that were originally developed in *Citizen and Subject*. The book provided the foundation for Mamdani's further work.

In 2001's *When Victims Become Killers: Colonialism, Nativism and the Genocide in Rwanda*, Mamdani places at center stage the ideas of ethnicity* and identity as a political construct* that originates in the colonial era. He goes on to examine how the politicization of ethnicity and identity have contributed to cycles of violence and genocide* in Rwanda since its independence.[2] His 2004 work *Good Muslim, Bad Muslim: America, the Cold War, and the Roots of Terror* delivers a non-Western perspective on the Cold War* and the rise of terrorism.[3] Here, Mamdani provides a historical analysis that criticizes the use of history by analogy,* just as he did in *Citizen and Subject*. In 2009's *Saviours and Survivors: Darfur, Politics, and the War on Terror* and his most recent publication, 2012's *Define and Rule: Native as Political Identity*, Mamdani focuses on another of the core themes of *Citizen and Subject*: the construction of identity and its roots.[4] Mamdani believes it is essential to understand this concept if we are to understand contemporary conflict and terrorism.

Summary

Citizen and Subject is an important contribution to the study of the contemporary African state. It delivers a provocative counterargument, or challenge, in the debate about the crisis of the African state in the late twentieth century. Whereas mainstream views emphasize that this crisis is homegrown, *Citizen and Subject* argues against this, explaining that the current crisis of the state is a consequence of the institutional legacy of colonialism. According to Mamdani, the colonial bifurcated state* has simply been reproduced by postcolonial regimes, instead of being done away with.

But *Citizen and Subject* is not only significant because of its main argument. In building this argument about the institutional legacy of colonialism, Mamdani also develops important notions about identity, ethnicity, and citizenship in the modern African state. These ideas have become influential in the study of African ethnic conflicts, state failure, and state reconstruction. *Citizen and Subject* also provides a valuable historical account of the contemporary African state, which is an important contribution to the historiography* of late twentieth-century Africa.

Citizen and Subject proved to be a major breakthrough for Mamdani's international career, earning him recognition as one of the world's foremost contemporary African scholars. In 1997, *Citizen and Subject* won the prestigious African Studies Association Herskovits[5] Prize for the best book published on Africa, and it has been named as one of the 100 best African books of the twentieth century.[6] In 2008, Mamdani was voted ninth top public intellectual by *Foreign Policy* magazine, confirming his status as an important voice of Africa.[7] He has published many more influential books since, but *Citizen and Subject* is likely to remain the key work in Mamdani's bibliography, principally because it set out the theoretical frame on which the rest of his writing developed.

NOTES

1   Mahmood Mamdani, "Making Sense of Political Violence in Postcolonial Africa," *Socialist Register* 39 (2003): 136.

2   Mahmood Mamdani, *When Victims Become Killers: Colonialism, Nativism and the Genocide in Rwanda* (Oxford: James Currey, 2001).

3   Mahmood Mamdani, *Good Muslim, Bad Muslim: America, the Cold War, and the Roots of Terror* (New York: Pantheon Books, 2004).

4   Mahmood Mamdani, *Saviours and Survivors: Darfur, Politics, and the War on Terror* (Cape Town: Human Sciences Research Council, 2009); Mahmood Mamdani, *Define and Rule: Native as Political Identity* (Cambridge, MA: Harvard University Press, 2012).

5   "J. Melville Herskovits Award," African Studies Association, accessed January 2, 2015, http://www.africanstudies.org/awards-prizes/herskovits-award.

6   "Africa's 100 best books of the 20th Century," African Studies Centre, accessed February 11, 2015, http://www.ascleiden.nl/content/webdossiers/africas-100-best-books-20th-century.

7   Anonymous, "The World's Top 20 Public Intellectuals," *Foreign Policy* 167 (2008): 54–7.

GLOSSARY

GLOSSARY OF TERMS

African impasse: a term used by Mahmood Mamdani to argue that that the African state is in a situation where progress is impossible. Since the end of colonialism, African states have been unable to reform local governance structures. For Mamdani, this is the main obstacle for successful democratization, as well as the core of problems associated with state failure in contemporary Africa.

African state: refers to the state as it exists in Africa. The term recognizes that, despite variations among countries, there are also important commonalities in the challenges they face.

Apartheid: the system of racial segregation under white minority rule that was in place in South Africa from 1948 to 1990.

Asian expulsion (Uganda): the period in 1972 when Ugandan President Idi Amin expelled all Asians from the country in an effort to place the economy in the hands of people Amin saw as "indigenous"—or native Ugandans.

Bifurcated state: a term coined by Mamdani referring to the legal and administrative division of the colonial state. The urban areas were subject to a modern European system of administration and law, while the rural areas were subject to a customary, or traditionally African, law and administration. While the urban areas were ruled through direct rule by the government, the rural areas were ruled through indirect rule, with government rule passing through traditional local authorities.

Civil society: a set of intermediate civil associations that are considered vital for a functioning democracy. Civil society organizations typically include Non-Governmental Organizations

(NGOs), Community Based Organizations (CBOs), trade unions, political parties, and churches and religious organizations.

CODESRIA: Council for the Development of Social Science Research in Africa. Founded in 1973 as an independent research organization that focuses primarily on social science research in Africa.

Cold War: the state of military, ideological, and political tension between the "Western Bloc," led by the United States, and the "Eastern bloc," led by the Soviet Union, that started after the end of World War II. It is referred to as a Cold War because despite high tension, there was never any direct fighting between the two superpowers, although several Cold War proxy wars occurred in Asia and Africa, most notably the Korean War (1950–53), the Vietnam War (1955–75) and the Angolan War (1975–91).

Colonialism, also referred to as colonial rule: the domination of territory and people by another country. Between the late nineteenth century and mid-twentieth century, almost the entire African continent was colonized by European powers.

Critical Theory: A range of theoretical approaches to society and culture, including neo-marxist, poststructuralist, postmodernist, postcolonial, and feminist critique.

Custom(ary): the domains that are traditional and defined by local custom and culture. In many postcolonial African states, legal systems were plural and traditional authorities were constitutionally provided with a role in the modern state system, thereby formally recognizing the customary in the modern state.

Darfur: a province in western Sudan, where a brutal civil war took place between 2003 and 2010 in which many civilians lost their lives.

Decentralized despotism: a term coined by Mamdani, by which he means the structures through which despotic colonial rule was mediated through tribal leadership, either freshly imposed or reconstituted as the hierarchy of the local state.

Democratization: The process of a transition from a non-democratic regime, such as authoritarian or dictatorial rule, to a democratic regime. Among other things, this involves designing a new constitution and legal framework, the building of new institutions of governance, and the organization of democratic elections.

Despotism: a form of government defined by the concentration of power in a single individual. A "despot" is usually understood to use their power cruelly.

Development theory: a collection of theories that explain how development, or social change, is best achieved, drawn from experiences of development, mainly in the Western world. Various forms of development theory, such as modernization theory, neo-liberal development theory, and dependency theory have been used to frame development strategies for postcolonial Africa.

Endogenise: to adapt a concept or theory internally.

Enough Project: a US-based project, founded in 2006, that aims to end genocide and crimes against humanity through research and giving voice to local communities in conflict areas.

Equatorial Africa: a geographical term that refers to the part of Africa that is crossed by the Equator.

Ethnicity: a marker of identity that draws on common ancestral, social, cultural, or national experience to define a group. In Africa, ethnicity is considered to be an important identity marker, more than in many other parts of the world.

Ethnic primordialism: an idea that holds that ethnicities are a natural, ancient phenomenon. This is as opposed to the social constructivist argument that holds that ethnicity is a social (or political) construct or invention.

Genocide: the systematic destruction of all members, or a significant part of, an identity group, such as a religious group, an ethnic group, or a racial group.

Good governance: a term used in international development to define how government institutions should be organized and function. It is criticized for being highly normative, and defined by subjective western practices.

Great Lakes region: a region of Africa referring geographically to the area in which Lake Victoria, Lake Tanganyika, Lake Albert, Lake Edward, and Lake Kivu are located, and the countries surrounding them. These countries are Uganda, Kenya, Tanzania, Rwanda, Burundi, and the Democratic Republic of Congo (DRC). The term "the conflict in the Great Lakes region" refers to the regional or cross-border conflict in the eastern DRC and its neighboring countries Rwanda, Burundi, and Uganda.

Historic–institutional approach: an analytical approach, central in *Citizen and Subject*, which centralizes the history of institutions and how these have shaped historic trajectories.

Historiography: the history of historical writing, and the history of a debate as it evolves over time

History by analogy: a historiographic approach that takes Western historic developments as the model against which those of Africa and other parts of the world are being measured.

Indigeneity: a condition describing what the United Nations defines as existing descendants of the peoples who inhabited the present territory of a country wholly or partially at the time when persons of a different culture or ethnic origin arrived there from other parts of the world, overcame them (by conquest, settlement, or other means), and reduced them to a non–dominant or colonial condition.

Indirect rule: a characteristic of colonial rule, often used to make a distinction between the French model of direct rule and the British model of indirect rule through local authorities.

Interdisciplinary: combining two or more academic disciplines in one research project in order to develop innovative research approaches that are cross-boundary.

Multidisciplinary: combining the insights obtained from two or more academic disciplines to come to a more comprehensive and holistic understanding.

Oral sources: information that is not recorded in written form, but is spoken. This includes stories, fables, sagas, songs, and oral history. Oral sources are an important source of information on societies that did not use any script, like most societies in pre-colonial Africa. It is, however, a contested source of information, mainly because of concerns about reliability and subjectivity.

Patrimonial rule/politics: Patrimonial rule or politics refers to a form of personal rule in which the ruler organizes his power similar to the management of a family or household. Patrimonial rule is typically organized around client–patron relations, and the distinction between the public domain and the private domain is often blurred, including in the management of finances.

Political economy: a school of thought that is founded on Marxist theory and focuses on the connection between the mode of production and the nature of power.

Political construct: an interpretation or understanding of something that has come about in support of a certain political objective.

Postcolonial state: a state that was previously colonized and that has obtained its political independence from colonial domination.

Postcolonial studies: a field of critical studies that originates in literary criticism. It is concerned with the discursive practices through which patterns of domination are produced and maintained.

Rwandan Genocide: in a period of 100 days in 1994, approximately 1 million Tutsi and moderate Hutu were killed by Hutu extremists. The aftermath of the genocide, especially the flow of refugees to neighboring countries and changes to Rwandan foreign policy, had a long-term impact on regional stability.

Save Darfur: an alliance of faith-based advocacy and human rights organizations, founded in 2004, that aims to bring an end to the violence in Darfur.

South African exceptionalism: a term explaining the "otherness" of South Africa in comparison to the rest of Africa. South Africa's historic trajectory differed so much from that of other parts of Africa—as a result of early colonization, the Boer settlers, white minority rule, and apartheid—that the country is often considered an "exception" in Sub-Saharan Africa. It is therefore often not included in generalized arguments about that area.

Soviet Union: a kind of "super state" that existed from 1922 to 1991, centered primarily on Russia and its neighbors in Eastern Europe and the northern half of Asia. It was the communist pole of the Cold War, with the United States as its main "rival".

State failure (also failed state): a term referring to the failure of a state to deliver its core obligations to its citizens. Indicators of state failure include a lack of territorial integrity and a lack of control over the territory by the state, the inability to provide security for its citizens, the inability to provide public services such as education and health care, and erosion of legitimacy of the political institutions.

Structural adjustment programs: programs initiated in the 1980s and 1990s, when many African countries were heavily indebted to international banks and were unable to repay their loans. The World Bank and International Monetary Fund provided loans and assistance to manage these debts under conditions that typically included devaluation, reducing the size of the public sector, and opening up the economy to foreign companies.

Subaltern studies: a field of studies that originated in the field of history, and was founded by the Subaltern Studies Group in India in the 1980s. Subaltern studies aims to return the people as subjects of their own history, and rejects the idea that they are passive participants in universal historic processes, such as the nationalist anti-colonial struggle.

Third Wave of Democratization: a movement that started in the mid-1970s with the collapse of military dictatorships in southern Europe, later followed by Eastern Europe and Africa at the end of the Cold War. It was dubbed the "Third Wave" after a first wave of democratization in the mid-nineteenth century, and a second wave following the end of World War II.

Traditional authorities: institutions of governance that base their authority on tradition or custom. In Africa, this generally refers to chiefs, kings, and traditional courts.

Tribalism: the use of tribes as units for analysis and sociopolitical organization.

Urban-rural divide: the notion of the persistent, deep, and multiple gaps between urban areas and rural areas in Africa. These gaps are seen in the economy, in politics, governance, levels of development, levels of education and literacy, job market, access to public services, and access to justice.

War on Terror: the international military campaign against Islamist terrorism and terrorist regimes by a coalition of countries and led by the United States. The term was first used by US President George W. Bush after the terrorist attacks on America on September 11, 2011.

PEOPLE MENTIONED IN THE TEXT

Idi Amin (1925–2003) was president of Uganda from 1971 to 1979. He came to power after a military coup and quickly installed a regime of terror. He was himself overthrown by a military coup.

Bertrand Badie (b. 1950) is a prominent political scientist, specializing in international relations, at the Institute for Political Science in Paris. His most important work is *The Imported State:The Westernisation of Political Order.*

Jean-François Bayart (b. 1950) is a prominent French sociologist at the University of Paris, Sorbonne. His work on contemporary African politics has been very influential.

Homi K. Bhabha (b. 1949) is professor of English language and literature at Harvard University. Bhabha is an important scholar in postcolonial studies, and has written influential theories on resistance by colonized people against their colonial oppressors.

Michel de Certeau (1925–86) was a French historian, psychoanalyst, and theorist. His most influential work is *The Practice of Everyday Life.*

Patrick Chabal (1951–2014) was an Africanist who was chair in African history and politics at Kings College, London. He is best known for his joint publication with Jean-Pascal Daloz, *Africa Works: Disorder as Political Instrument.*

Frederick Cooper (b. 1947) is professor of history at New York University, and specializes in the history of African colonization and decolonization.

Jean Copans (b. 1942) is a French anthropologist and sociologist and a specialist on francophone Africa.

Basil Davidson (1914–2010) was a prominent British historian and Africanist. He published extensively on pre-colonial, colonial, and postcolonial African history. His most important work is *The Black Man's Burden: Africa and the Curse of the Nation-State*.

Edward Evan Evans-Pritchard (1902–73) was an English anthropologist who developed the field of social anthropology, working with Oxford University. He is best know for his work on the Azande and Nuer people: *Witchcraft, Oracles and Magic among the Azande* and *The Nuer: A Description of the Modes of Livelihood and Political Institutions of a Nilotic People*.

Frantz Fanon (1926–61) was a Martinique born, Afro-French psychiatrist, revolutionary, philosopher, and author, who defended the right of colonized people to use violence as a means to achieve liberation. His most important works are *The Wretched of the Earth* and *Black Skin, White Masks*.

Michel Foucault (1926–84) was a French philosopher. An important part of his work is concerned with the relation between power and knowledge, and forms of social control.

Jeffrey Herbst (b. 1961) is an American political scientist. He was president of Colgate University, New York, from 2010 to 2015. Herbst's book, *States and Power in Africa*, was critically acclaimed.

Yoweri Museveni (b. 1944) is President of Uganda since 1986. He is the leader of the National Resistance Movement, and came to power after a military rebellion.

Milton Obote (1924–2005) was prime minister (1962–70) and twice president (1966–71, 1980–85) of Uganda. He was overthrown by Idi Amin in a military coup in 1971, but regained power in 1980 with the help of Tanzanian military support. In 1985 he was forced out of office again.

John Prendergast (b. 1963) is an American human rights activist. He is director of the Enough Project, a Non-Governmental Organization against genocide and crimes against humanity.

Edward Said (1935–2003) was a Palestinian American literary and cultural critic. His most influential work is *Orientalism*, which was foundational for the field of postcolonial critique.

Gayatri Chakravorty Spivak (b. 1942) is an Indian literary theorist and philosopher who teaches at Columbia University. Her most important work is the 1988 essay "Can the Subaltern Speak?"

Jan Vansina (b. 1929) is a Belgian historian and anthropologist working on the people of the Central African region. Vansina's work on the oral history of African people has been important for the development of historiography of pre-colonial Africa. His best known work is *Paths in the Rainforest*.

Crawford Young (b. 1931) is a political scientist, specializing in African politics. He is best known for his landmark study of the Zairian state (co-authored with Thomas Turner), *The Zairian State in Comparative Perspective*, and his work on the colonial state in Africa, *The African Colonial State in Comparative Perspective*.

WORKS CITED

WORKS CITED

Abrahamsen, Rita. *Disciplining Democracy: Development Discourse and Good Governance in Africa*. London: Zed Books, 2000.

Africa Progress Panel. *Jobs, Justice and Equity: Seizing Opportunities in Times of Global Change. Africa Progress Report 2012.* Africa Progress Panel, 2012.

African Studies Association. "J. Melville Herskovits Award." Accessed January 2, 2015. http://www.africanstudies.org/awards-prizes/herskovits-award.

African Studies Centre. "Africa's 100 best books of the 20th Century." Accessed February 11, 2015. http://www.ascleiden.nl/content/webdossiers/africas-100-best-books-20th-century.

Anderson, Benedict. *Imagined Communities: Reflections on the Origin and Spread of Nationalism.* New York: Verso, 1991.

Anonymous. "The World's Top 20 Public Intellectuals," *Foreign Policy* 167 (2008), 54–7.

Ansprenger, Franz. "Review of *Citizen and Subject*," *The International Journal of African Historical Studies* 30, no. 3 (1997).

Austen, Ralph A. "Review of *Citizen and Subject*." *Law and History Review* 17, no. 2 (1999): 406–8.

Badie, Bertrand. *The Imported State: The Westernisation of Political Order*. Translated by Claudia Royal. Stanford, CA: Stanford University Press, 2000.

Baker, Bruce. "The Class of 1990: How Have the Autocratic Leaders of Sub-Saharan Africa Fared under Democratisation?" *Third World Quarterly* 19, no. 1 (1998): 115–27.

Bates, Robert H. *When Things Fell Apart: State Failure in Late-Century Africa.* Cambridge: Cambridge University Press, 2008.

Bayart, Jean-François. *The State in Africa: The Politics of the Belly*. London: Polity, 1993.

Les études postcoloniales: Un carnaval académique. Paris: Karthala, 2010.

"L'historicité de l'État importé," in *La greffe de l'état,* edited by J.-F. Bayart. Paris: Karthala, 1996.

Bayart, Jean-François, Stephen Ellis, and Béatrice Hibou. *The Criminalisation of the State in Africa*. Oxford: James Currey, 1999.

Berman, Bruce J. "Ethnicity, Patronage and the African State: The Politics of Uncivil Nationalism." *African Affairs* 97, no. 388 (1998): 305–41.

Berman, Bruce J., and John Lonsdale. *Unhappy Valley: Conflict in Kenya and Africa*. Oxford: James Currey, 1992.

Bhabha, Homi K. *The Location of Culture*. London: Routledge, 2004.

Bratton, Michael, and Nicolas van de Walle. *Democratic Experiments in Africa: Regime Transitions in Comparative Perspective*. Cambridge: Cambridge University Press, 1997.

Certeau, Michel de. *The Practice of Everyday Life*. Translated by Steven Rendall. Berkeley, CA: University of California Press, 1984.

Chabal, Patrick. *Power in Africa: An Essay in Political Interpretation*. New York: St Martin's Press, 1992.

Africa: The Politics of Suffering and Smiling. London: Zed Books, 2009.

Chabal, Patrick, and Jean-Pascal Daloz. *Africa Works: Disorder as Political Instrument*. Oxford: James Currey, 1999.

Chandra, Kanchan. "Cumulative Findings in the Study of Ethnic Politics." *APSA-CP Newsletter* 12, no. 1 (2001): 7–11.

Cooper, Frederick. "Review of *Citizen and Subject*." *International Labor and Working-Class History* 52 (1997): 156–60.

Colonialism in Question: Theory, Knowledge, History. Berkeley, CA: University of California Press, 2005.

Copans, Jean. "Review of *Citizen and Subject*." *Transformation* 36 (1998): 102–5.

Davidson, Basil. *The Black Man's Burden: Africa and the Curse of the Nation-State*. Oxford: James Currey, 1992.

Das, Anil Kumar. "The Reluctant Democrat: Museveni and the Future of Democracy in Uganda." *Africa Quarterly* 39, no. 4 (1999): 61–78.

Democracy Now! "Mahmood Mamdani on Darfur: The Politics of Naming: Genocide, Civil War, Insurgency." Accessed February 16, 2015. http://www.democracynow.org/2007/6/4/mahmood_mamdani_on_darfur_the_politics.

Devarajan, Shantayanan and Wolfgang Fengler. "Africa's Economic Boom: Why the Pessimists and the Optimists Are Both Right." *Foreign Affairs* (May/June 2013): 15.

Douglas, Stuart. "Review of *Citizen and Subject*." *American Anthropologist* 100, no. 2 (1998): 550–51.

Englebert, Pierre. "The Contemporary African State: Neither African nor State." *Third World Quarterly* 18, no. 4 (1997): 767–75.

Englebert, Pierre and Kevin C. Dunn. *Inside African Politics*. Boulder, CO: Lynne Rienner, 2013.

Evans-Pritchard, Edward E. *Witchcraft, Oracles, and magic Among the Azande*. Oxford: Oxford University Press, 1937.

The Nuer: A Description of the Modes of Livelihood and Political Institutions of a Nilotic People. Oxford: Clarendon Press, 1940.

Fanon, Frantz. *The Wretched of the Earth*. London: Penguin, 1967.

Foucault, Michel. *Discipline and Punish: The Birth of the Prison*. London: Penguin, 1991.

Gerhart, Gail M. "Citizen and Subject: Contemporary Africa and the Legacy of Late Colonialism." *Foreign Affairs* 28 (May/June 1997). Accessed April 28, 2015. http://www.foreignaffairs.com/articles/52843/gail-m-gerhart/citizen-and-subject-contemporary-africa-and-the-legacy-of-late-c.

Graaff, Johann. "Pandering to Pedagogy or Consumed by Content: Brief Thoughts on Mahmood Mamdani's 'Teaching at the Post-Apartheid University of Cape Town'." *Social Dynamics* 24, no. 2 (1998): 76–85.

Greenstein, Ran. "Review of *Citizen and Subject*." *African Sociological Review* 1, no. 2 (1997): 105–16.

Whitney, Joel. "The Genocide Myth: Joel Whitney Interviews Mahmood Mamdani, May 12, 2009." *Guernica*. Accessed February 16, 2015. https://www.guernicamag.com/interviews/the_genocide_myth/.

Hall, Martin. "Teaching Africa at the Post-Apartheid University of Cape Town: A Response." *Social Dynamics* 24, no. 2 (1998): 40–62.

"'Bantu Education'? A Reply to Mahmood Mamdani." *Social Dynamics* 24, no. 2 (1998): 86–92.

Harsch, Ernest. "African States in Social Historical Context." *Sociological Forum* 12, no. 4 (1997): 671–9.

Hartman, Nadia. "Discussion of Certain Aspects of Mamdani's Paper: Teaching Africa at the Post-Apartheid University of Cape Town." *Social Dynamics* 24, no. 2 (1998): 33–9.

Herbst, Jeffrey. "Review of *Citizen and Subject*." *Annals of the American Academy of Political and Social Science* 554 (1997): 216–17.

States and Power in Africa: Comparative Lessons in Authority and Control. Princeton, NJ: Princeton University Press, 2000.

Huntington, Samuel P. *The Third Wave: Democratization in the Late Twentieth Century*. Norman, OK: University of Oklahoma Press, 1991.

Hyden, Goran. *African Politics in Comparative Perspective*. Cambridge: Cambridge University Press, 2006.

Idahosa, P. L. E. "Review of *Citizen and Subject*." *International History Review* 20, no. 2 (1998): 493–6.

Jeffries, Richard. "The state, structural adjustment and good government in Africa." *Journal of Commonwealth and Comparative Politics* 31, no. 1 (1993): 20–35.

Kaarsholm, Preben. "Review of *Citizen and Subject*." *Journal of Southern African Studies* 23, no. 2 (1997): 386–8.

Kamola, Isaac A. "Pursuing Excellence in a World-Class University: the Mamdani Affairs and the Politics of Global Higher Education." *Journal of Higher Education in Africa* 9, nos. 1 and 2 (2011): 121–42.

Kapoor, Ilan. *The Postcolonial Politics of Development*. New York: Routledge, 2008.

Kimber, Charlie. "Interview: Mahmood Mamdani on Darfur." *Socialist Review* 337 (2009).

Leach, Adam. "Review of *Citizen and Subject*." *Development in Practice* 7, no. 3 (1997): 314–15.

"Review of *Citizen and Subject*." *Review of African Political Economy* 24, no. 72 (1997): 295–7.

Lonsdale, John. "Power and Resistance." *Journal of African History* 38, no. 3 (1997): 520–22.

Lynch, Gabrielle and Gordon Crawford. "Democratization in Africa 1990–2010: An Assessment." *Democratization* 18, no. 2 (2011): 275–310.

Mamdani, Mahmood. *From Citizen to Refugee: Ugandan Asians Come to Britain*. London: Frances Pinter, 1973.

Politics and Class Formation in Uganda. London: Heinemann Educational, 1976.

"Analysing the Agrarian Question: the Case of a Buganda Village." *Mawazo* 5, no. 3 (1983): 47–64.

"Forms of Labour and Accumulation of Capital: Analysis of a Village in Lango, Northern Uganda." *Mawazo* 5, no. 4 (1983): 44–65.

"Extreme But Not Exceptional: Towards an Analysis of the Agrarian Question in Uganda." *Journal of Peasant Studies* 14, no. 2 (1987): 191–225.

"The Ugandan Asian Expulsion: Twenty Years After." *Journal of Refugee Studies* 6, no. 3 (1993): 265–73.

African Studies in Social Movements and Democracy. Dakar: CODESRIA, 1995.

Citizen and Subject: Contemporary Africa and the Legacy of Late Colonialism. Princeton, NJ: Princeton University Press, 1996.

"A Response to Comments." *African Sociological Review* 1, no. 2 (1997): 145–55.

"Is African Studies to be Turned Into a New Home for Bantu Education at UCT?" Text of remarks by Professor Mahmood Mamdani at the Seminar on the Africa Core of the Foundation Course for the Faculty of Social Sciences and Humanities, University of Cape Town, April 22, 1998.

"Teaching Africa at the Post-Apartheid University of Cape Town: A Critical View of the 'Introduction to Africa' Core Course in the Social Science and Humanities Faculty's Foundation Semester, 1998." *Social Dynamics* 24, no. 2 (1998): 1–32.

"Is African Studies to be Turned Into a New Home for Bantu Education at UCT?" *Social Dynamics* 24, no 2 (1998): 63–75.

Understanding the Crisis in Kivu: Report of the CODESRIA Mission to the Democratic Republic of Congo, September 1997. Dakar: CODESRIA, 1998.

"Commentary: Mahmood Mamdani Responds to Jean Copans' Review in *Transformation* 36." *Transformation* 39 (1999): 97–101.

When Victims Become Killers: Colonialism, Nativism and the Genocide in Rwanda. Oxford: James Currey, 2001.

"Making Sense of Political Violence in Postcolonial Africa." *Socialist Register* 39 (2003): 132–51.

Good Muslim, Bad Muslim: America, the Cold War, and the Roots of Terror. New York: Pantheon Books, 2004.

Saviours and Survivors: Darfur, Politics, and the War on Terror. Cape Town: Human Sciences Research Council, 2009.

Define and Rule: Native as Political Identity. Cambridge, MA: Harvard University Press, 2012.

"Prof. Mahmood Mamdani and John Prendergast, 'The Darfur Debate.'" April 14, 2009, [25:14-25:39]. Accessed January 11, 2015. https://www.youtube.com/watch?v=yGOpfH_5_pY.

McLean, Iain and Alistair McMillan, *Oxford Concise Dictionary of Politics.* Oxford: Oxford University Press, 2003.

Ministry of Local Government. *Report of the Commission of Inquiry into the Local Government System.* Kampala, Uganda, June 1987.

Msinde Aseka, Eric, Bill Freund, Ran Greenstein, Ulf Himmelstrand, Martin Legassick, Julius E. Nyang'oro, and Eddie Webster. "Review Symposium: Mahmood Mamdani and the Analysis of African Society." *African Sociological Review* 1, no. 2 (1997): 96–144.

Muller, Johann. "Editorial Introduction." *Social Dynamics* 24, no. 2 (1998): 1–6.

Murray, Martin. "Configuring the Trajectory of African Political History." *Canadian Journal of African Studies* 34, no. 2 (2000): 376–86.

Ndegwa, Stephen N. "Review of *Citizen and Subject*." *Africa Today* 45, no. 2 (1998): 264–6.

Nustad, Knut. "Review of *Citizen and Subject*." *Journal of Peace Research* 35, no. 5 (1998): 650.

Nyang'oro, Julius E. "The Evolving Role of the African State under Structural Adjustment." In *Beyond Structural Adjustment in Africa: the Political Economy of Sustainable and Democratic Development,* edited by Julius E. Nyang'oro and Timothy M. Shaw, 11–27 (New York: Praeger, 1992).

Owosu, Maxwell. "Democracy and Africa? A View from the Village." *Journal of Modern African Studies* 30, no. 3 (1992): 369–396.

Prendergast, John. "Prof. Mahmood Mamdani and John Prendergast, 'The Darfur Debate.'" April 14, 2009. Accessed January 11, 2015. https://www.youtube.com/watch?v=yGOpfH_5_pY.

Prunier, Gerard. *The Rwanda Crisis: History of a Genocide*. London: Hurst, 1997.

Przeworski, Adam, Michael Alvarez, José Antonio Cheibub and Fernando Limongi. "What Makes Democracies Endure?" *Journal of Democracy* 7, no. 1 (1996): 39–55.

Ranger, Terence. "The Invention of Tradition in Colonial Africa." In *The Invention of Tradition*, edited by E. J. Hobsbawm and Terence Ranger, 211–62. Cambridge: Cambridge University Press, 1993.

Reno, William. *Warlord Politics and African States*. Boulder, CO: Lynne Rienner, 1998.

Robertson, Charles, Yvonne Mhango, and Michael Moran. *The Fastest Billion: the Story Behind Africa's Economic Revolution.* London: Renaissance Capital, 2012.

Ross, Robert. *A Concise History of South Africa. Second Edition.* Cambridge: Cambridge University Press, 2008.

Rotberg, Robert I. "The Failure and Collapse of Nation-States: Breakdown, Prevention, and Repair." In *When States Fail: Causes and Consequences*, edited by Robert I. Rotberg, 1–49. Princeton, NJ: Princeton University Press, 2004.

Said, Edward W. *Orientalism*. London: Penguin, 2003.

Schedler, Andreas. "The Menu of Manipulation." *Journal of Democracy* 13, no. 2 (2002): 36–50.

Shaw, Carolyn Martin. "Review of *Citizen and Subject*," *American Ethnologist* 25, no. 3 (1998): 531–2.

Spears, Ian S. Review of *After Colonialism* and *Citizen and Subject*. *Canadian Journal of African Studies* 30, no. 1 (1997): 177–9.

Spivak, Gayatri Chakravorty. "Can the Subaltern Speak?" In *Marxism and the Interpretation of Culture*, edited by Cary Nelson and Lawrence Grossberg, 271–313. Urbana, IL: University of Illinois Press, 1988.

Taylor, Ian. *Africa Rising? BRICS—Diversifying Dependency.* London: James Currey, 2014.

Tignor, Robert L. "Review of *Citizen and Subject*." *American Historical Review* 102, no. 5 (1997): 1541.

Van den Berghe, Pierre. "Does Race Matter?" In *Ethnicity*, edited by John Hutchinson and Anthony D. Smith. Oxford: Oxford University Press, 1996.

Vansina, Jan. *Oral Tradition as History*. London: James Currey, 1985.

Paths in the Rainforest: Toward a History of Political Tradition in Equatorial Africa. Madison, WI: University of Wisconsin Press, 1990.

Warscapes. "In Conversation with Mahmood Mamdani, by Bakhti Bhakti Shringarpure, July 15, 2013." Accessed February 16, 2015. http://www.warscapes.com/conversations/conversation-mahmood-mamdani.

Wiseman, John A. "Review of *Citizen and Subject*." *Journal of Developing Areas* 31, no. 2 (1997): 273–5.

Youé, Chris. "Mamdani's History." *Canadian Journal of African Studies* 34, no. 2 (2000): 397–408.

Young, Crawford. "The Third Wave of Democratization in Africa: Ambiguities and Contradictions." In *State, Conflict and Democracy,* edited by Richard Joseph. Boulder, CO: Lynne Rienner, 1999.

"The End of the Post-Colonial State in Africa? Reflections on Changing African Political Dimensions." *African Affairs* 103 (2004): 23–49.

Young, Tom. "Review Article: The State and Politics in Africa." *Journal of Southern African Studies* 25, no. 1 (1999): 149–54.

THE MACAT LIBRARY
BY DISCIPLINE

The Macat Library By Discipline

AFRICANA STUDIES

Chinua Achebe's *An Image of Africa: Racism in Conrad's Heart of Darkness*
W. E. B. Du Bois's *The Souls of Black Folk*
Zora Neale Huston's *Characteristics of Negro Expression*
Martin Luther King Jr's *Why We Can't Wait*
Toni Morrison's *Playing in the Dark: Whiteness in the American Literary Imagination*

ANTHROPOLOGY

Arjun Appadurai's *Modernity at Large: Cultural Dimensions of Globalisation*
Philippe Ariès's *Centuries of Childhood*
Franz Boas's *Race, Language and Culture*
Kim Chan & Renée Mauborgne's *Blue Ocean Strategy*
Jared Diamond's *Guns, Germs & Steel: the Fate of Human Societies*
Jared Diamond's *Collapse: How Societies Choose to Fail or Survive*
E. E. Evans-Pritchard's *Witchcraft, Oracles and Magic Among the Azande*
James Ferguson's *The Anti-Politics Machine*
Clifford Geertz's *The Interpretation of Cultures*
David Graeber's *Debt: the First 5000 Years*
Karen Ho's *Liquidated: An Ethnography of Wall Street*
Geert Hofstede's *Culture's Consequences: Comparing Values, Behaviors, Institutes and Organizations across Nations*
Claude Lévi-Strauss's *Structural Anthropology*
Jay Macleod's *Ain't No Makin' It: Aspirations and Attainment in a Low-Income Neighborhood*
Saba Mahmood's *The Politics of Piety: The Islamic Revival and the Feminist Subject*
Marcel Mauss's *The Gift*

BUSINESS

Jean Lave & Etienne Wenger's *Situated Learning*
Theodore Levitt's *Marketing Myopia*
Burton G. Malkiel's *A Random Walk Down Wall Street*
Douglas McGregor's *The Human Side of Enterprise*
Michael Porter's *Competitive Strategy: Creating and Sustaining Superior Performance*
John Kotter's *Leading Change*
C. K. Prahalad & Gary Hamel's *The Core Competence of the Corporation*

CRIMINOLOGY

Michelle Alexander's *The New Jim Crow: Mass Incarceration in the Age of Colorblindness*
Michael R. Gottfredson & Travis Hirschi's *A General Theory of Crime*
Richard Herrnstein & Charles A. Murray's *The Bell Curve: Intelligence and Class Structure in American Life*
Elizabeth Loftus's *Eyewitness Testimony*
Jay Macleod's *Ain't No Makin' It: Aspirations and Attainment in a Low-Income Neighborhood*
Philip Zimbardo's *The Lucifer Effect*

ECONOMICS

Janet Abu-Lughod's *Before European Hegemony*
Ha-Joon Chang's *Kicking Away the Ladder*
David Brion Davis's *The Problem of Slavery in the Age of Revolution*
Milton Friedman's *The Role of Monetary Policy*
Milton Friedman's *Capitalism and Freedom*
David Graeber's *Debt: the First 5000 Years*
Friedrich Hayek's *The Road to Serfdom*
Karen Ho's *Liquidated: An Ethnography of Wall Street*

John Maynard Keynes's *The General Theory of Employment, Interest and Money*
Charles P. Kindleberger's *Manias, Panics and Crashes*
Robert Lucas's *Why Doesn't Capital Flow from Rich to Poor Countries?*
Burton G. Malkiel's *A Random Walk Down Wall Street*
Thomas Robert Malthus's *An Essay on the Principle of Population*
Karl Marx's *Capital*
Thomas Piketty's *Capital in the Twenty-First Century*
Amartya Sen's *Development as Freedom*
Adam Smith's *The Wealth of Nations*
Nassim Nicholas Taleb's *The Black Swan: The Impact of the Highly Improbable*
Amos Tversky's & Daniel Kahneman's *Judgment under Uncertainty: Heuristics and Biases*
Mahbub Ul Haq's *Reflections on Human Development*
Max Weber's *The Protestant Ethic and the Spirit of Capitalism*

FEMINISM AND GENDER STUDIES

Judith Butler's *Gender Trouble*
Simone De Beauvoir's *The Second Sex*
Michel Foucault's *History of Sexuality*
Betty Friedan's *The Feminine Mystique*
Saba Mahmood's *The Politics of Piety: The Islamic Revival and the Feminist Subject*
Joan Wallach Scott's *Gender and the Politics of History*
Mary Wollstonecraft's *A Vindication of the Rights of Woman*
Virginia Woolf's *A Room of One's Own*

GEOGRAPHY

The Brundtland Report's *Our Common Future*
Rachel Carson's *Silent Spring*
Charles Darwin's *On the Origin of Species*
James Ferguson's *The Anti-Politics Machine*
Jane Jacobs's *The Death and Life of Great American Cities*
James Lovelock's *Gaia: A New Look at Life on Earth*
Amartya Sen's *Development as Freedom*
Mathis Wackernagel & William Rees's *Our Ecological Footprint*

HISTORY

Janet Abu-Lughod's *Before European Hegemony*
Benedict Anderson's *Imagined Communities*
Bernard Bailyn's *The Ideological Origins of the American Revolution*
Hanna Batatu's *The Old Social Classes And The Revolutionary Movements Of Iraq*
Christopher Browning's *Ordinary Men: Reserve Police Batallion 101 and the Final Solution in Poland*
Edmund Burke's *Reflections on the Revolution in France*
William Cronon's *Nature's Metropolis: Chicago And The Great West*
Alfred W. Crosby's *The Columbian Exchange*
Hamid Dabashi's *Iran: A People Interrupted*
David Brion Davis's *The Problem of Slavery in the Age of Revolution*
Nathalie Zemon Davis's *The Return of Martin Guerre*
Jared Diamond's *Guns, Germs & Steel: the Fate of Human Societies*
Frank Dikotter's *Mao's Great Famine*
John W Dower's *War Without Mercy: Race And Power In The Pacific War*
W. E. B. Du Bois's *The Souls of Black Folk*
Richard J. Evans's *In Defence of History*
Lucien Febvre's *The Problem of Unbelief in the 16th Century*
Sheila Fitzpatrick's *Everyday Stalinism*

The Macat Library By Discipline

Eric Foner's *Reconstruction: America's Unfinished Revolution, 1863-1877*
Michel Foucault's *Discipline and Punish*
Michel Foucault's *History of Sexuality*
Francis Fukuyama's *The End of History and the Last Man*
John Lewis Gaddis's *We Now Know: Rethinking Cold War History*
Ernest Gellner's *Nations and Nationalism*
Eugene Genovese's *Roll, Jordan, Roll: The World the Slaves Made*
Carlo Ginzburg's *The Night Battles*
Daniel Goldhagen's *Hitler's Willing Executioners*
Jack Goldstone's *Revolution and Rebellion in the Early Modern World*
Antonio Gramsci's *The Prison Notebooks*
Alexander Hamilton, John Jay & James Madison's *The Federalist Papers*
Christopher Hill's *The World Turned Upside Down*
Carole Hillenbrand's *The Crusades: Islamic Perspectives*
Thomas Hobbes's *Leviathan*
Eric Hobsbawm's *The Age Of Revolution*
John A. Hobson's *Imperialism: A Study*
Albert Hourani's *History of the Arab Peoples*
Samuel P. Huntington's *The Clash of Civilizations and the Remaking of World Order*
C. L. R. James's *The Black Jacobins*
Tony Judt's *Postwar: A History of Europe Since 1945*
Ernst Kantorowicz's *The King's Two Bodies: A Study in Medieval Political Theology*
Paul Kennedy's *The Rise and Fall of the Great Powers*
Ian Kershaw's *The "Hitler Myth": Image and Reality in the Third Reich*
John Maynard Keynes's *The General Theory of Employment, Interest and Money*
Charles P. Kindleberger's *Manias, Panics and Crashes*
Martin Luther King Jr's *Why We Can't Wait*
Henry Kissinger's *World Order: Reflections on the Character of Nations and the Course of History*
Thomas Kuhn's *The Structure of Scientific Revolutions*
Georges Lefebvre's *The Coming of the French Revolution*
John Locke's *Two Treatises of Government*
Niccolò Machiavelli's *The Prince*
Thomas Robert Malthus's *An Essay on the Principle of Population*
Mahmood Mamdani's *Citizen and Subject: Contemporary Africa And The Legacy Of Late Colonialism*
Karl Marx's *Capital*
Stanley Milgram's *Obedience to Authority*
John Stuart Mill's *On Liberty*
Thomas Paine's *Common Sense*
Thomas Paine's *Rights of Man*
Geoffrey Parker's *Global Crisis: War, Climate Change and Catastrophe in the Seventeenth Century*
Jonathan Riley-Smith's *The First Crusade and the Idea of Crusading*
Jean-Jacques Rousseau's *The Social Contract*
Joan Wallach Scott's *Gender and the Politics of History*
Theda Skocpol's *States and Social Revolutions*
Adam Smith's *The Wealth of Nations*
Timothy Snyder's *Bloodlands: Europe Between Hitler and Stalin*
Sun Tzu's *The Art of War*
Keith Thomas's *Religion and the Decline of Magic*
Thucydides's *The History of the Peloponnesian War*
Frederick Jackson Turner's *The Significance of the Frontier in American History*
Odd Arne Westad's *The Global Cold War: Third World Interventions And The Making Of Our Times*

LITERATURE

Chinua Achebe's *An Image of Africa: Racism in Conrad's Heart of Darkness*
Roland Barthes's *Mythologies*
Homi K. Bhabha's *The Location of Culture*
Judith Butler's *Gender Trouble*
Simone De Beauvoir's *The Second Sex*
Ferdinand De Saussure's *Course in General Linguistics*
T. S. Eliot's *The Sacred Wood: Essays on Poetry and Criticism*
Zora Neale Huston's *Characteristics of Negro Expression*
Toni Morrison's *Playing in the Dark: Whiteness in the American Literary Imagination*
Edward Said's *Orientalism*
Gayatri Chakravorty Spivak's *Can the Subaltern Speak?*
Mary Wollstonecraft's *A Vindication of the Rights of Women*
Virginia Woolf's *A Room of One's Own*

PHILOSOPHY

Elizabeth Anscombe's *Modern Moral Philosophy*
Hannah Arendt's *The Human Condition*
Aristotle's *Metaphysics*
Aristotle's *Nicomachean Ethics*
Edmund Gettier's *Is Justified True Belief Knowledge?*
Georg Wilhelm Friedrich Hegel's *Phenomenology of Spirit*
David Hume's *Dialogues Concerning Natural Religion*
David Hume's *The Enquiry for Human Understanding*
Immanuel Kant's *Religion within the Boundaries of Mere Reason*
Immanuel Kant's *Critique of Pure Reason*
Søren Kierkegaard's *The Sickness Unto Death*
Søren Kierkegaard's *Fear and Trembling*
C. S. Lewis's *The Abolition of Man*
Alasdair MacIntyre's *After Virtue*
Marcus Aurelius's *Meditations*
Friedrich Nietzsche's *On the Genealogy of Morality*
Friedrich Nietzsche's *Beyond Good and Evil*
Plato's *Republic*
Plato's *Symposium*
Jean-Jacques Rousseau's *The Social Contract*
Gilbert Ryle's *The Concept of Mind*
Baruch Spinoza's *Ethics*
Sun Tzu's *The Art of War*
Ludwig Wittgenstein's *Philosophical Investigations*

POLITICS

Benedict Anderson's *Imagined Communities*
Aristotle's *Politics*
Bernard Bailyn's *The Ideological Origins of the American Revolution*
Edmund Burke's *Reflections on the Revolution in France*
John C. Calhoun's *A Disquisition on Government*
Ha-Joon Chang's *Kicking Away the Ladder*
Hamid Dabashi's *Iran: A People Interrupted*
Hamid Dabashi's *Theology of Discontent: The Ideological Foundation of the Islamic Revolution in Iran*
Robert Dahl's *Democracy and its Critics*
Robert Dahl's *Who Governs?*
David Brion Davis's *The Problem of Slavery in the Age of Revolution*

Alexis De Tocqueville's *Democracy in America*
James Ferguson's *The Anti-Politics Machine*
Frank Dikotter's *Mao's Great Famine*
Sheila Fitzpatrick's *Everyday Stalinism*
Eric Foner's *Reconstruction: America's Unfinished Revolution, 1863-1877*
Milton Friedman's *Capitalism and Freedom*
Francis Fukuyama's *The End of History and the Last Man*
John Lewis Gaddis's *We Now Know: Rethinking Cold War History*
Ernest Gellner's *Nations and Nationalism*
David Graeber's *Debt: the First 5000 Years*
Antonio Gramsci's *The Prison Notebooks*
Alexander Hamilton, John Jay & James Madison's *The Federalist Papers*
Friedrich Hayek's *The Road to Serfdom*
Christopher Hill's *The World Turned Upside Down*
Thomas Hobbes's *Leviathan*
John A. Hobson's *Imperialism: A Study*
Samuel P. Huntington's *The Clash of Civilizations and the Remaking of World Order*
Tony Judt's *Postwar: A History of Europe Since 1945*
David C. Kang's *China Rising: Peace, Power and Order in East Asia*
Paul Kennedy's *The Rise and Fall of Great Powers*
Robert Keohane's *After Hegemony*
Martin Luther King Jr.'s *Why We Can't Wait*
Henry Kissinger's *World Order: Reflections on the Character of Nations and the Course of History*
John Locke's *Two Treatises of Government*
Niccolò Machiavelli's *The Prince*
Thomas Robert Malthus's *An Essay on the Principle of Population*
Mahmood Mamdani's *Citizen and Subject: Contemporary Africa And The Legacy Of Late Colonialism*
Karl Marx's *Capital*
John Stuart Mill's *On Liberty*
John Stuart Mill's *Utilitarianism*
Hans Morgenthau's *Politics Among Nations*
Thomas Paine's *Common Sense*
Thomas Paine's *Rights of Man*
Thomas Piketty's *Capital in the Twenty-First Century*
Robert D. Putman's *Bowling Alone*
John Rawls's *Theory of Justice*
Jean-Jacques Rousseau's *The Social Contract*
Theda Skocpol's *States and Social Revolutions*
Adam Smith's *The Wealth of Nations*
Sun Tzu's *The Art of War*
Henry David Thoreau's *Civil Disobedience*
Thucydides's *The History of the Peloponnesian War*
Kenneth Waltz's *Theory of International Politics*
Max Weber's *Politics as a Vocation*
Odd Arne Westad's *The Global Cold War: Third World Interventions And The Making Of Our Times*

POSTCOLONIAL STUDIES

Roland Barthes's *Mythologies*
Frantz Fanon's *Black Skin, White Masks*
Homi K. Bhabha's *The Location of Culture*
Gustavo Gutiérrez's *A Theology of Liberation*
Edward Said's *Orientalism*
Gayatri Chakravorty Spivak's *Can the Subaltern Speak?*

PSYCHOLOGY

Gordon Allport's *The Nature of Prejudice*
Alan Baddeley & Graham Hitch's *Aggression: A Social Learning Analysis*
Albert Bandura's *Aggression: A Social Learning Analysis*
Leon Festinger's *A Theory of Cognitive Dissonance*
Sigmund Freud's *The Interpretation of Dreams*
Betty Friedan's *The Feminine Mystique*
Michael R. Gottfredson & Travis Hirschi's *A General Theory of Crime*
Eric Hoffer's *The True Believer: Thoughts on the Nature of Mass Movements*
William James's *Principles of Psychology*
Elizabeth Loftus's *Eyewitness Testimony*
A. H. Maslow's *A Theory of Human Motivation*
Stanley Milgram's *Obedience to Authority*
Steven Pinker's *The Better Angels of Our Nature*
Oliver Sacks's *The Man Who Mistook His Wife For a Hat*
Richard Thaler & Cass Sunstein's *Nudge: Improving Decisions About Health, Wealth and Happiness*
Amos Tversky's *Judgment under Uncertainty: Heuristics and Biases*
Philip Zimbardo's *The Lucifer Effect*

SCIENCE

Rachel Carson's *Silent Spring*
William Cronon's *Nature's Metropolis: Chicago And The Great West*
Alfred W. Crosby's *The Columbian Exchange*
Charles Darwin's *On the Origin of Species*
Richard Dawkin's *The Selfish Gene*
Thomas Kuhn's *The Structure of Scientific Revolutions*
Geoffrey Parker's *Global Crisis: War, Climate Change and Catastrophe in the Seventeenth Century*
Mathis Wackernagel & William Rees's *Our Ecological Footprint*

SOCIOLOGY

Michelle Alexander's *The New Jim Crow: Mass Incarceration in the Age of Colorblindness*
Gordon Allport's *The Nature of Prejudice*
Albert Bandura's *Aggression: A Social Learning Analysis*
Hanna Batatu's *The Old Social Classes And The Revolutionary Movements Of Iraq*
Ha-Joon Chang's *Kicking Away the Ladder*
W. E. B. Du Bois's *The Souls of Black Folk*
Émile Durkheim's *On Suicide*
Frantz Fanon's *Black Skin, White Masks*
Frantz Fanon's *The Wretched of the Earth*
Eric Foner's *Reconstruction: America's Unfinished Revolution, 1863-1877*
Eugene Genovese's *Roll, Jordan, Roll: The World the Slaves Made*
Jack Goldstone's *Revolution and Rebellion in the Early Modern World*
Antonio Gramsci's *The Prison Notebooks*
Richard Herrnstein & Charles A Murray's *The Bell Curve: Intelligence and Class Structure in American Life*
Eric Hoffer's *The True Believer: Thoughts on the Nature of Mass Movements*
Jane Jacobs's *The Death and Life of Great American Cities*
Robert Lucas's *Why Doesn't Capital Flow from Rich to Poor Countries?*
Jay Macleod's *Ain't No Makin' It: Aspirations and Attainment in a Low Income Neighborhood*
Elaine May's *Homeward Bound: American Families in the Cold War Era*
Douglas McGregor's *The Human Side of Enterprise*
C. Wright Mills's *The Sociological Imagination*

Thomas Piketty's *Capital in the Twenty-First Century*
Robert D. Putman's *Bowling Alone*
David Riesman's *The Lonely Crowd: A Study of the Changing American Character*
Edward Said's *Orientalism*
Joan Wallach Scott's *Gender and the Politics of History*
Theda Skocpol's *States and Social Revolutions*
Max Weber's *The Protestant Ethic and the Spirit of Capitalism*

THEOLOGY

Augustine's *Confessions*
Benedict's *Rule of St Benedict*
Gustavo Gutiérrez's *A Theology of Liberation*
Carole Hillenbrand's *The Crusades: Islamic Perspectives*
David Hume's *Dialogues Concerning Natural Religion*
Immanuel Kant's *Religion within the Boundaries of Mere Reason*
Ernst Kantorowicz's *The King's Two Bodies: A Study in Medieval Political Theology*
Søren Kierkegaard's *The Sickness Unto Death*
C. S. Lewis's *The Abolition of Man*
Saba Mahmood's *The Politics of Piety: The Islamic Revival and the Feminist Subjec*t
Baruch Spinoza's *Ethics*
Keith Thomas's *Religion and the Decline of Magic*

COMING SOON

Chris Argyris's *The Individual and the Organisation*
Seyla Benhabib's *The Rights of Others*
Walter Benjamin's *The Work Of Art in the Age of Mechanical Reproduction*
John Berger's *Ways of Seeing*
Pierre Bourdieu's *Outline of a Theory of Practice*
Mary Douglas's *Purity and Danger*
Roland Dworkin's *Taking Rights Seriously*
James G. March's *Exploration and Exploitation in Organisational Learning*
Ikujiro Nonaka's *A Dynamic Theory of Organizational Knowledge Creation*
Griselda Pollock's *Vision and Difference*
Amartya Sen's *Inequality Re-Examined*
Susan Sontag's *On Photography*
Yasser Tabbaa's *The Transformation of Islamic Art*
Ludwig von Mises's *Theory of Money and Credit*

Macat Disciplines

Access the greatest ideas and thinkers across entire disciplines, including

AFRICANA STUDIES

Chinua Achebe's *An Image of Africa: Racism in Conrad's Heart of Darkness*

W. E. B. Du Bois's *The Souls of Black Folk*

Zora Neale Hurston's *Characteristics of Negro Expression*

Martin Luther King Jr.'s *Why We Can't Wait*

Toni Morrison's *Playing in the Dark: Whiteness in the American Literary Imagination*

Macat analyses are available from all good bookshops and libraries.

Access hundreds of analyses through one, multimedia tool.
Join free for one month **library.macat.com**

Macat Disciplines

Access the greatest ideas and thinkers across entire disciplines, including

FEMINISM, GENDER AND QUEER STUDIES

Simone De Beauvoir's
The Second Sex

Michel Foucault's
History of Sexuality

Betty Friedan's
The Feminine Mystique

Saba Mahmood's
*The Politics of Piety:
The Islamic Revival and
the Feminist Subject*

Joan Wallach Scott's
*Gender and the
Politics of History*

Mary Wollstonecraft's
*A Vindication of the
Rights of Woman*

Virginia Woolf's
A Room of One's Own

Judith Butler's
Gender Trouble

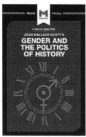

Macat Disciplines

*Access the greatest ideas and thinkers
across entire disciplines, including*

INEQUALITY

Ha-Joon Chang's, *Kicking Away the Ladder*

David Graeber's, *Debt: The First 5000 Years*

Robert E. Lucas's, *Why Doesn't Capital Flow from
Rich To Poor Countries?*

Thomas Piketty's, *Capital in the Twenty-First Century*

Amartya Sen's, *Inequality Re-Examined*

Mahbub Ul Haq's, *Reflections on Human Development*

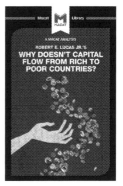

Macat analyses are available from all good bookshops and libraries.

Access hundreds of analyses through one, multimedia tool.
Join free for one month **library.macat.com**

Macat Disciplines

*Access the greatest ideas and thinkers
across entire disciplines, including*

CRIMINOLOGY

Michelle Alexander's
*The New Jim Crow:
Mass Incarceration in the
Age of Colorblindness*

**Michael R. Gottfredson
& Travis Hirschi's**
A General Theory of Crime

Elizabeth Loftus's
Eyewitness Testimony

**Richard Herrnstein
& Charles A. Murray's**
*The Bell Curve: Intelligence and
Class Structure in American Life*

Jay Macleod's
*Ain't No Makin' It:
Aspirations and Attainment in a
Low-Income Neighborhood*

Philip Zimbardo's
The Lucifer Effect

Macat Disciplines

Access the greatest ideas and thinkers across entire disciplines, including

MACAT

Postcolonial Studies

Roland Barthes's *Mythologies*
Frantz Fanon's *Black Skin, White Masks*
Homi K. Bhabha's *The Location of Culture*
Gustavo Gutiérrez's *A Theology of Liberation*
Edward Said's *Orientalism*
Gayatri Chakravorty Spivak's *Can the Subaltern Speak?*

Macat analyses are available from all good bookshops and libraries.

Access hundreds of analyses through one, multimedia tool.
Join free for one month **library.macat.com**

Macat Disciplines

Access the greatest ideas and thinkers across entire disciplines, including

GLOBALIZATION

Arjun Appadurai's, *Modernity at Large: Cultural Dimensions of Globalisation*

James Ferguson's, *The Anti-Politics Machine*

Geert Hofstede's, *Culture's Consequences*

Amartya Sen's, *Development as Freedom*

Macat analyses are available from all good bookshops and libraries.

Access hundreds of analyses through one, multimedia tool.
Join free for one month **library.macat.com**

Macat Pairs

Analyse historical and modern issues from opposite sides of an argument. Pairs include:

HOW TO RUN AN ECONOMY

John Maynard Keynes's
The General Theory OF Employment, Interest and Money

Classical economics suggests that market economies are self-correcting in times of recession or depression, and tend toward full employment and output. But English economist John Maynard Keynes disagrees.

In his ground-breaking 1936 study *The General Theory*, Keynes argues that traditional economics has misunderstood the causes of unemployment. Employment is not determined by the price of labor; it is directly linked to demand. Keynes believes market economies are by nature unstable, and so require government intervention. Spurred on by the social catastrophe of the Great Depression of the 1930s, he sets out to revolutionize the way the world thinks

Milton Friedman's
The Role of Monetary Policy

Friedman's 1968 paper changed the course of economic theory. In just 17 pages, he demolished existing theory and outlined an effective alternate monetary policy designed to secure 'high employment, stable prices and rapid growth.'

Friedman demonstrated that monetary policy plays a vital role in broader economic stability and argued that economists got their monetary policy wrong in the 1950s and 1960s by misunderstanding the relationship between inflation and unemployment. Previous generations of economists had believed that governments could permanently decrease unemployment by permitting inflation—and vice versa. Friedman's most original contribution was to show that this supposed trade-off is an illusion that only works in the short term.

Macat analyses are available from all good bookshops and libraries.

Access hundreds of analyses through one, multimedia tool. Join free for one month **library.macat.com**

Macat Disciplines

*Access the greatest ideas and thinkers
across entire disciplines, including*

THE FUTURE OF DEMOCRACY

  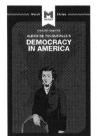 

Robert A. Dahl's, *Democracy and Its Critics*
Robert A. Dahl's, *Who Governs?*
Alexis De Toqueville's, *Democracy in America*
Niccolò Machiavelli's, *The Prince*
John Stuart Mill's, *On Liberty*
Robert D. Putnam's, *Bowling Alone*
Jean-Jacques Rousseau's, *The Social Contract*
Henry David Thoreau's, *Civil Disobedience*

Macat Disciplines

Access the greatest ideas and thinkers across entire disciplines, including

TOTALITARIANISM

Sheila Fitzpatrick's, *Everyday Stalinism*
Ian Kershaw's, *The "Hitler Myth"*
Timothy Snyder's, *Bloodlands*

Printed in the United States
by Baker & Taylor Publisher Services